M000106373

MOVE YOUR MOUNTAINS

The Secret to Breakthrough

Dwain Wolfe

All rights reserved. No part of this publication may be reproduced, stored in a retrieval system, or transmitted in any form or by any means – electronic, mechanical, photocopying, recording or otherwise- without the prior written permission of the publisher. The only exception is a brief quotation printed review. All Bible references are from the New American Standard Bible unless otherwise noted.

Verses marked NASB are from the New American Standard Bible, Copywrite the Lockman foundation. Verses marked NIV are taken from the New International Version. Copywrite by Biblica, Inc. Used by permission of Zondervan.

Dwain Wolfe
Visit my website at www.dwainwolfe.org

Printed in the United States of America

First Printing: December 2018
Restored Life Press
5600 Valley Ave E
Fife, WA 98424

"Before I knew a thing anything about moving mountains the Lord started increasing my faith and granting me a greater and greater gift of faith. At the time I don't know if I knew it was Him, but it was later revealed to me that He was at the center of revelation that was giving me faith for the impossible. I pray that as you read this material your eyes will be opened and you will see what very few know. I'm convinced that few Christians know how to pray to move mountains, but this is about to change. This book contains dynamite power to change your world and the world around you. Following this book, read my book on Move Their Mountain: The Secret to Effective Intercession. God bless you as you read, may you never be the same again'

-Dwain Wolfe

This book is dedicated to wonderful wife, Joel, who has stood by me since 1983. Though we've experienced challenges in life, she's followed me with faith and developed into an amazing minister of the gospel. She's also been a rock of strength in raising our four amazing children. Over the years I've had opportunity to practice all of the spiritual principles you'll read about in this book on her and my children. We are becoming a family of mountain movers. Thank you "love bug" for throwing your energy and gifts into my calling and becoming the best wife I could have hoped for. Thank you also to New Horizon Church of Tacoma Washington. As founding and lead pastor you've let me practice on you as the Lord was leading me. Though I've been imperfect you've accepted my leadership, mistakes and all.

About Dwain Wolfe

Pastor Dwain Wolfe has served as a pastor since 1983 and is the founding pastor of New Horizon Church in Tacoma Washington. New Horizon is a non-denominational Christian church. He is a graduate of Northwest University, father of four amazing children and husband of Joel Robertson Wolfe since 1983. In the early 90's he began a ministry to the oppressed, troubled, abused and addicted. He is the author of several books on successful Christian living and the founder of Restored Life. Restored Life is a transformational ministry benefiting many Christians with freedom and restoration. He has been blessed to see many mountains of trouble move for him, for others and for the Kingdom of God. Write him at nhccwolfe@gmail.com or contact him through New Horizon Church.

ACKNOWLEDGMENTS

Many thanks to so many who have allowed me to grow in ministry and become the Son that Father ordained. Special thanks to my wife and children who have allowed me to spend countless hours coaching the amazing people of God. I believe that you sharing me with the body of Christ will pay off in the lives of transformed people and a better world. Thank you for your sacrifice and investment in others. You are the best family ever and I'm so very grateful. Many thanks to my wife Joel, who keeps supporting the call of God on my life, through thick and thin. Many thanks to an amazing team that supports me; Joe Sims, Craig Lapenski, Bill Barnett, Heidi Leitheiser, Will Johnson, Mandy Kaplan Treadwell, Zach Sanders Byron Leavitt, Jasmine Mattson, Carla Pieplow and many more. You too are living examples of this theology and each of you bless me.

CONTENTS

MOVE YOUR MOUNTAINS

The Secret to Breakthrough

Dwain Wolfe

THE MIRACLE – THE RAIN STOPPED

You are about to read how to deploy the central key to mountain moving prayer, the hidden key that will revolutionize your "prayer" life. Through the proper deployment of this key, a new level of joy in the will be yours again. I believe this key is a missing key, overlooked by much of the body of Christ. That's why I've taken the time to put it down on paper and make it a topic to provoke the body of Christ. The principles of moving mountains have totally revolutionized my life.

I'll tell you now, it does not involve praying for hours and hour, worshiping for hours, praying more fervently or fasting. These factors are valid and have relevance for sure, but without what I'm about to unveil in this book these factors might not produce a mountain moving result.

WHAT IS A MOUNTAIN MOVER?

I would submit to you that when Jesus said you can move a mountain it was both a reality and a figure of speech.   Rarely would we need to move a physical mountain. In addition, we might note that throughout the bible we don't see any historical figure ever move a natural mountain. But we do see some other amazing feats of faith, every bit as impressive as the moving of a mountain. We see the sun made to stand still, we see rain stopped for three years, we see hungry lions unable to eat a man, we see a river stopped upstream, we see an axe head float, we see walls of a city fall down and much more.

So, what about a mountain? What is a mountain? A mountain in this story told by Jesus represented something huge, something immoveable, something that without God would be impossible. Let me give you an example out of the physical realm– under the topic of reigning in life. The year was 2012 and the season was rain, rain and more rain but we got a miracle. I live in the N where it rains a lot during the fall and winter.

In the Seattle Tacoma area we receive 39 inches of rain each year. When the fall falls upon us it's going to be wet. On Halloween night in 2012 our church was again going to host an outdoor event called Trunk or Treat. We'd set up around 30 cars in the parking lot all with a fun game event in each trunk where they'd also give out candy and build relationships. This was a big event for our church family to connect with the community. We'd had as many as 800 attend this event and therefore it gives us exposure to the loving community of our church body. This particular year the event was look bleak and there was much talk in and among the staff that we should cancel. The reason? Rain. The forecast for October 31 was rain, 100% precipitation. It was pouring all week leading up to this event, but a month before the event I announced it would be dry.

As we got closer to the event, I felt more faith and I went so far as to say it would be dry between 4:30 and 8:30 pm. Then as the gift of faith was developing within me, I said there would be a clearing and the sun would come out. I give the credit to Jesus for I feel that faith is a gift.

The gift of faith coming out of my mouth was contrary to the many voices of doom and gloom. Many of our church members wanted us to surrender to the weather and call off the event, but I would not agree. I continued to encourage them that I had put in an order for the weather. Finally, Wednesday Oct 31 came, and it was raining all day. Several were asking if we should try to use Eze – up Canopies and just make a go of it with all the rain falling.

In the natural it looked terrible and if I would have just heeded the warnings, we could have made preparations. It was looking like we'd be in a big mess since due to pastor we hadn't gathering enough canopies or solutions and we hadn't canceled. In the midst of this I continued to say, "it's going to dry up at 4:30." I'm blessed to have such a compliant team willing to take risk with me because as we were preparing for that evening, just at 4:30 the rain stopped over our City and over the church. Most of the volunteers continued to set up their spot, but a few noticed. Staff members shot me grins and thumbs up. High 5's abounded. Shortly after 4:30 the clouds parted, and the sun came out. God had met me with a miracle. At 8:30 just as we closed down and were putting the fair away, the rains started back in.

Glory to God, we witnessed a miracle. How did it happen? The keys this book will unlock the answer. I'll revisit this story later and tell you the exact details but suffice it to say it happened through an application of faith and authority in the spirit realm. That story and its fulfillment is what this book is all about. We'll seek to show you in this book how to move mountains with faith and authority much like Mark described about Jesus in Mark 11.

We'll show you that you have the same power and authority to do what I've just described and so much more!

I want you to see that Christians are called and anointed by God to exercise the authority He's given us to reign in life, rule over the earth, dominate Satan and establish the Kingdom of God. This is what Sons of God do. This is what the early believers did to spread the gospel and establish the Kingdom of God. This is how to live as a Son of God and see the manifest power of God work through you. You and I are called to walk in HIS authority. This book is to encourage you to make these kinds of things a present reality for every day.

Reign in Life
Rule over the earth
Dominate Satan
Reverse the curse
Establish the Kingdom of God

When you find the power of God at your disposal and bear much fruit, then you will find renewed joy and fulfillment in your walk with God. The truth unveiled in this book will revolutionize your life and many that you'll tell. What you are about to read will cause you to become a **mountain mover** in God.

I personally have seen "mountain moving prayer" work to heal the sick, catch swordfish in ocean waters, stop rain storms, drive out devils, grow the church, curb evil plans, bring calm to my children, bring forth financial supply and totally change a city government that had no clear evangelical witness. I could go on listing what I've seen this "mountain moving" prayer key accomplish. Using this prayer key is how I live every single day of my life. It's how God has ordained us to live!

Now I'll admit, I didn't grow up with this theology, and maybe you're just like me. I grew up in a traditional denominational church and in that group we believed God and we prayed, but we didn't understand our authority. If we got a breakthrough it was almost a mysterious accident because we really didn't know how we got the breakthrough.

LET'S LOOK AT THIS RADICAL PASSAGE!

And the seventy returned with joy, saying, "Lord, even the demons are subject to us in Your name." And He said to them, "I was watching Satan fall from heaven like lightning. "Behold, I have given you authority to tread upon serpents and scorpions, and over all the power of the enemy, and nothing shall injure you.
Luke 10:17-19

Do you long for to live in the hour of experiencing the things described in this passage in by Brother Luke? Jesus had just anointed seventy disciples and sent them out two by two. This passage encapsulates what happened when they returned.

Imagine with me the setting of this story and situation. Hundreds had been witnessing the miracles and the power of God being manifested through Jesus and they were totally awestruck. With authority He spoke to demons and they obeyed! They had never seen such authority.

> *Luke 4:36 And amazement came upon them all, and they began discussing with one another saying, "What is this message? For with authority and power He commands the unclean spirits, and they come out."*

Now in this instance, found in Luke 10, He gathered them up for what was something like a modern-day church service and gave them an invitation. He might have said to them, "would you all like to help me in this mission?" "if you would, then come forward and I'll lay hands on you."

Little did they realize He was going to send them out to minister. They didn't understand much yet, but they knew that Jesus had authority over everything. Seventy of the disciples came forward and let Him touch them. Maybe He anointed them with oil and prayed over them maybe He just laid his hands on them. Either way we know <u>He gave them a temporary taste of His authority</u>.

Then Luke records what happened next this way, "then He sent them out to heal the sick and cast out devils."

Later these same disciples return to Jesus and in verse 17. Doctor Luke records that when they returned to Jesus, they returned with joy. They returned with joy because what He told them to do actually worked. They might have left the prayer meeting with fear, but they returned with joy because the demons and sicknesses were subject to them.

How did they discover that demons and sicknesses were subject to them unless something visible happened to give proof of this fact? What had taken place through these deputized disciples that lit them up like candles with joy? What had them so stoked that Jesus had to calm them down when they returned. If Jesus must calm you down, you are really stoked up about something.

Consider this fact, that rarely do we have this problem in the body of Christ, if you know what I'm talking about. What they were excited about was that they, each of them had experienced a visible demonstration of the power of God like they had never seen before, except through Jesus. They had gone out into their community and they saw God move with signs and wonders through their prayers. They had gone out in and cast out demons and cast out sickness and God worked with them to confirm the anointing authority of Jesus. Imagine the sheer excitement and joy of being one of those disciples.

When they returned, Jesus told them that when they were doing what **He** sent them out to do, "Satan's kingdom was falling." And He said to them, *"I was watching Satan fall from heaven like lightning."* Yes, through their ministry Satan's power was falling, Satan's rule was falling, Satan's kingdom was falling.

Now consider this truth: that Satan is enthroned by all the evil he has wrought against mankind. The bondage and harm and sickness and oppression make a throne for him. Evil is the embodiment of his rule or dominion, the manifestation and assurance. The word kingdom means; the dominion of a King. Satan has a kingdom, and it is called in the Bible the Kingdom of Darkness. The good news is that it can be torn down. When we, the members of the body of Christ, do what God has called us to do, standing in the authority of Christ Jesus, then Satan's kingdom falls...not completely, but to the degree that we dispossess it. No wonder they came back with joy.

Joy is one of missing elements of the modern church. Not joy at the espresso bar because the coffee shot was just perfect. Not joy in the foyer, because we just saw our best friend. Not joy because the worship band has such a sweet sound. But genuine joy over being used of God in such a powerful way it can't be described. Joy that's so over the top our minister has to calm us down.

You've got to admit that this is extremely uncommon in the body of Christ. I've been raised in the church as a minister's kid and now pastoring all of my adult life and I can count on two hands how many Christians I've seen with this much joy, and I believe the lack has been because of unanswered prayer. Now let's go back to this story. Jesus was telling the disciples; the Kingdom of God grows up and increases at the same time and to the same degree that the Kingdom of darkness is shrinking. The shrinkage in this day, as it was in that, is dependent up us healing the sick, casting out demons and helping those oppressed by the devil.

> Luke 11:20 But if I drive out demons by the
> *finger* of *God*, then the kingdom of *God*
> has come upon you.

We must see that we are called and anointed by God to exercise the authority He's given us to destroy the kingdom of Satan and establish the Kingdom of God. This is what sons of God do. This practice session is what the early believers did to spread the gospel and establish the Kingdom of God. This is how to live as a son of God and see the manifest power of God work through you. You and I are called to walk in HIS authority.

This book is to encourage you to make the Luke 10 experience a present reality for every day. When you find the power of God at your disposal and bear much fruit, then you will find renewed joy. The truth unveiled in this book will revolutionize your life and many that you'll tell.

> *What you are about to read will cause you to become a mountain mover in God and through prayer.*

Just as those 70 went out and moved some mountains and shook some things up, you too will become a shaker and mover for God. I truly believe that herein is the key to conquering Satan and his cleverly devised kingdom.

Remember Jesus saw Satan falling from heaven like lightning when these disciples did something that he told them to do. It's when they stood in the authority of Jesus and commanded things to change. I personally have seen "mountain moving prayer" work to heal the sick, catch swordfish in ocean waters, stop rain storms, drive out devils, grow the church, curb evil plans, bring calm to my children, bring forth financial supply and totally change a city government that had no clear evangelical witness.

I could go on listing what I've seen this "mountain moving" prayer key accomplish. Using this prayer key is how I live every single day of my life. It's how God has ordained us to live!

Now I'll warn you, I didn't grow up with this theology under my belt. I grew up in a traditional denomination. In that group we believed God and we prayed, but we didn't understand our authority, and to my knowledge we didn't properly exercise our authority. We didn't understand our place as <u>God's deputies</u>.

All of our prayers were aimed toward God in order to get or receive a reaction or solution from Him.

For example, we'd pray, "God please help us over smoking and drinking." Or, "Dear Father, please help us overcome this fear that come upon us." Or, "Dear God, please take away this cancer."

And in a similar fashion, "God, please do this and God please do that..."

"Dear Lord, please take this evil habit away from me."

"Dear Lord, please stop the rain that will ruin our crops if it comes."

If God didn't do what we prayed, we explained this failure to receive the answer, with the saying, "it must not have been God's will."

Many times, we'd finish our prayer request with, "nevertheless, thy will be done." Or we'd finish a prayer of petition or request with a discussion on how we'd know God's will by what happened next.

For example, if the person was healed, that healing would reveal God's will. If the person's fear went away, we'd know that was God's will. If it didn't happen as we prayed, then we'd know that God intended for the person to "deal" with the "negative" situation and that the situation must be "God's will" and that they were probably supposed to "learn something from it."

Over the last 25 years God has shown me many truths concerning answered prayer and I've attempted to describe this in this writing. He's used many teachers of faith to encourage me to search the scriptures, as well as teaching me through real life situations and experimentation. I've practiced the principles that I'm espousing in this book and seen God work hundreds of times. I've dealt with demons and I've dealt with nature. I've also found that what I learned in the arena of deliverance ministry could be expanded to other areas. I learned clearly that I have delegated authority over demons and over nature. Deliverance ministry is a foundation to exercising authority in all realms. Once you begin to see the authority you have over demons you begin to get a glimpse of your authority as a son of God.

One example is how God has changed our City, since He has given us delegated authority there.

CAN A CITY BE CHANGED?

James 1:2-5 Consider it all joy, my brethren, when you encounter various trials, knowing that the testing of your faith produces endurance. And let endurance have its perfect result, that you may be perfect and complete, lacking in nothing. But if any of you lacks wisdom, let him ask of God, who gives to all men generously and without reproach, and it will be given to him.

Take courage Christian, He knows the name of your mountain too and He knows how to move it.

Have you ever stood before a mountain that's greater than you? We stood at such a place when we answered God's call to start a church in a small town in Washington State. I want to encourage your faith by sharing about a manifestation of change and favor that came upon us after much prayer over our City and its stance against our church.

My wife and I planted our church toward the end of 1991. Planting a church is a challenging job by any measurement, but especially in a city where the true gospel is not welcomed.

Some great Christian leaders in America these days don't believe in spiritual warfare. They don't believe that there can be a difference in certain locations to the effect of the gospel. They say that since the Lord has won the battle it's easy to take any territory for the Kingdom of God. I would say they haven't faced a real battle yet, nor do they understand spiritual warfare. It could be that they are blessed to minister in a territory where someone else already broke the demonic resistance. Maybe you are in a place where there are powers of darkness entrenched against you and your mission. If so, be encouraged, you can win a mighty victory. We could tell from the beginning that our assignment was different. I'm not a spooky person and I wasn't going to be discouraged, but there was something stale and demonic hovering in the atmosphere of our little town.

It started when we first set out to find a place for our new church to meet. Our first place to look was the local "community center. When we secured the rental for the local community center, the manager told me then that four other pastors had tried to start a church in the same community center only to give up and move on. That sounded strange, but we pressed ahead anyway.

Over time it became clearer that there was a stance against the charismatic evangelical church in our City.

This negative stance had insidiously permeated government, the school district and the influential business owners of our City. Therefore, we faced opposition everywhere and at every turn. The warfare wasn't just limited to "spiritual". In the City, the opposition was overt and many times obvious. We felt like foreigners who weren't welcome.

Other ministers in the local area were contentious, jealous and hateful. City permits were denied, we were locked out of our rentals, we were kicked out of buildings, buildings were closed to leases, rents were doubled, leases were disallowed, engineering firms fought us over trumped up legalities, neighbors hated us and the school district opposed us. It seemed that there was a new brush fire to be put out each and every week.

Inwardly and within our church body we also felt the strain of spiritual warfare. Division and selfish ambition in the leadership was normal for during that period. For seven years we experienced strife, division, jealousy and competition within the eldership team. When an elder would leave the church people would make false accusations against my wife, myself and the elders that remained.

In that process other people would leave the church in bitterness or misunderstanding. We literally felt like we were living in our own Frank Peretti novel. "This Present Darkness" was a present reality every single day. This and more all went on for 8 years before we saw the first breakthrough. The beginning of breakthroughs came in 1998. It first became evident that a breakthrough was upon us when changes started taking place in the City. In 1998 the City Council voted to change the form of government from a Mayor led government to a City Manager led government. We felt that this was great news for our church and a time to **move a mountain**.

Let me explain. Since the inception of our City, an elected Mayor and City Council had led the government. Also, as far as was overtly evident the City had been opposed to churches like ours and had worked behind the scene to discourage their presence. Many other pastors had come to the City and started churches only to leave discouraged and beat up. Other churches in the neighboring communities were small and under strong levels of oppression. Only one church had flourished in our community and the City government leaders, since the inception of the City, had belonged to that church.

We were seekers of God and God's answers. We knew we were called to this mission. We knew we had heard God's voice and we were not going to give up. We were determined, and we were going to see this mountain moved. God knew the name of our mountain.

He knew what stood before us and opposed us. We knew if we sought Him, we would receive wisdom from Him.

> *James 1:2-5 Consider it all joy, my brethren, when you encounter various trials, knowing that the testing of your faith produces endurance. And let endurance have its perfect result, that you may be perfect and complete, lacking in nothing. But if any of you lacks wisdom, let him ask of God, who gives to all men generously and without reproach, and it will be given to him.*

Take courage Christian, He knows the name of your mountain too and He knows how to move it. As we were seeking God, He opened up some revelation. Through a dream in 1993 God showed my wife and I that a demon spirit, a "strong man" or prince in the spirit realm, was the key to the opposition, hindrance and slow growth of our church. He showed us we were being opposed in the spirit realm by a demon entrenched in the leadership and activities of our City.

This revelation was a great help and encouragement to us, but we didn't yet know how to overcome this spirit. We kept seeking the Lord on who this spirit was and how to overcome it. Then one day it came...one day while seeking the Lord, He revealed to me one that the name of this "stronghold" over our City was "Babylon", and there were two spiritual powers that needed to be confronted.

The powers could be named "Bel" and "Marduk" just as it was in the book of Jeremiah. Through this revelation God was enabling us to direct our prayers to the top of the food chain, instead of the bottom.

I began to understand what Paul wrote in Ephesians chapter six, that our war was not with flesh and blood, though it looked like it often.

Our battle was with spiritual power and things that were going on in the spirit realm. These activities in the spirit realm were influencing the nature events of life. If we made flesh and blood our target, we'd never get our breakthroughs. But if we made the spiritual powers our target of prayer, we'd begin to get victory

> *Ephesians 6:11 Put on the full armor of*
> *God, that you may be able to stand firm*
> *against the schemes of the devil. 12 For*
> *our struggle is not against flesh and blood,*
> *but against the rulers, against the powers,*
> *against the world forces of this darkness,*
> *against the spiritual forces of wickedness*
> *in the heavenly places.*

I began to see that there is no difference between driving a demon out of a person or driving it out of a territory. If I can do the one, I can do the other. In prayer one day, the Lord gave me Jeremiah 50 and told me to begin to <u>vocally declare the spirit of Babylon, Bel and Marduk destroyed and crushed under the power of Jesus Christ</u>.

> *Jeremiah 50:2 "Declare and proclaim*
> *among the nations. Proclaim it and lift up*
> *a standard. Do not conceal it but say,*
> *'Babylon has been captured, Bel has been*
> *put to shame, Marduk has been shattered;*
> *Her images have been put to shame, her*
> *idols have been shattered.*

He made it clear that we weren't to oppose the people who were against us, they were not ultimately our enemies (Ephesians 6:10-12). We were called to demolish the evil principalities of spiritual wickedness. Our enemies were in the spirit realm over the City and working through people in the City.

This kind of "warfare" prayer began with real clarity in 1993. As we began to do this and continued, slowly we began to see breakthroughs. Remember evil spirits must be driven out. This means that we keep pressing until we win!

In the years following 1993 I would call our people to prayer for the community. We would have strategic meetings just for the purpose of breakthrough. We'd regularly gather at the City Hall building at night and pray outside the doors. We would anoint the City Hall building with oil and claim the City for God. We really believed God would intervene for us as we prayed.

During those days and for years we would have late night prayer meetings, early morning prayer meetings, home group prayer meetings, three-day prayer meetings and weekend prayer meetings.

At each of these prayer meetings we would command Satan to give up the City and his dominion over it. We called upon God to raise up righteousness and the righteous. We fasted and declared the Word of God over the community over and over again. Then we had our first big breakthrough!

In the fall of 1999 we heard that the City was ready to look outside to hire a City manager to run the affairs of the City. I felt lead to ask God for a Christian city manager. When I went to praying, I felt an even more aggressive tug on my heart. I felt in my spirit and in my desire that we should ask God for a Charismatic Christian manager.

God led me to believe that a Spirit filled Christian would have complete empathy for our plight in the city. When I questioned the Lord, and protested praying this way, I felt impressed to press in and press through. This prayer for a Spirit filled Christian manager was something that was being **born of God.**

> *I John 5:4 For whatever is born of God*
> *overcomes the world; and this is the*
> *victory that has overcome the world-- our*
> *faith.*

Knowing God's will was a relief and it meant I didn't have to convince Him. This too is a key to spiritual breakthrough. Once you know God's will you can bind the powers that oppose it and loose God's power to fulfill it.

I now needed believers to join with me in declaring God's will into the atmosphere of the spirit realm. I believed that the combined prayers of the saints would break down the resistance of demons sooner or later. Together our prayer warriors begin to lift this request up to God and also declare its fulfillment.

To condense this story, in May of 2000 a new City manager came to work for our City. He moved from another city where he was the city manager and had faithfully attended a Spirit filled - Pentecostal church. Praise God! He was the only born-again Christian interviewed by the City. He had a strong Christian testimony and openly served God. He was immediately interested in our church and its status.

Within two months of him coming to the City and coming on staff he called and asked for a meeting with me. When we came to the City Hall to meet with him, he said that he had read through out file and was dismayed. He wanted to know what he could do to help our church get established.

We suddenly had a city manager that understood us and was not trying to keep us from growth and progress. We saw more breakthroughs in the next three months after he came on the job than in all the eight years that preceded his coming. God had turned things around for us in the City.

Now all of that being said, God was also teaching us about spiritual warfare. Much of the progress in our church and many of the breakthroughs like this one have come as a result of prayer.

- Not just by rubbing shoulders with the right people.
- Not just by getting out there and sharing my opinion.
- Not just by serving the community or in the community.
- Not by our membership on the Chamber of Commerce.

Though we've done all these afore mentioned things, they didn't bring the ultimate breakthroughs. By praying the things God has shown us to pray and saying the things God told us to say God gave us the breakthroughs.

> *Proverbs 21: 31 The horse is prepared for the day of battle, But victory belongs to the LORD.*

God is still a **mountain moving God** and He wants His Church to start trusting in Him to move mountains, big mountains. He wants us to start trusting in His ability to work through our prayers like never before. God is moving us into **mountain moving faith.**

Not just

- "pay the bill faith"
- "buy a car faith"
- "fix the marriage faith"
- "911 faith"

God is calling us to take the principles of dominion revealed in Luke 10 and change our Cities. Cities and communities and cultures can be changed, demons will fall like lightning and churches can grow and flourish like He intended.

Now, you might find this doctrine rubbing you the wrong way from time to time.

If you do, then you might be misunderstanding my thesis. Go back and read it again. Go through the scriptures again.

This is not a "boss God around" book. This is a "find out what God is doing and saying" then confess it and do it. This is what Jesus did.

Don't stay in your current understanding and write this off. The theme of this book is not typically popular in religious circles, but then again neither was Jesus. Please don't throw this out if it doesn't fit your past, your tradition, your religious upbringing or doctrines. God is wanting to break the Church into new realms with prayer and prophecy. It starts with saying what God says about your life, your marriage, your work, your health, your conversion and everything in life.

As the children of Israel came out of the land of promise they came to the land of Canaan. The land of Canaan was a goodly land and it was their inheritance.

God told them He was going to take them into this land and defeat the enemies for them and give them this land of milk and honey.

He brought them to the land and told them to send in 12 spies to spy out the land, one from each tribe of Israel. The spies returned with samples from the land of milk and hone and when they returned 10 of the spies had a evil report, but 2 had an good report. The good report was a report that agreed with God. A confession that said what God had said.

A good report is when we boldly agree with God.

They weren't in the majority, but they agreed with God. This is most often the way God chooses to exercise His sovereignty in the earth. He looks for someone who will agree with Him and confess what He has desired for them. When He finds someone who will agree with His will then He will bring it to pass for them.

Ten of the spies had a evil report, it was evil because it contradicted God's word and will, therefore He called it a evil report. They said, "there are giants in the land and the giants are too big for us, thus we are not able to go up and possess the land." They saw themselves as worms and therefore so did the giants.

> *Numbers 13:32 So they gave out to the sons of Israel a bad report of the land which they had spied out, saying, "The land through which we have gone, in spying it out, is a land that devours its inhabitants; and all the people whom we saw in it are men of great size. "There also we saw the Nephilim (the sons of Anak are part of the Nephilim); and we became like grasshoppers in our own sight, and so we were in their sight.*

"What was the result of this evil confession or report? God declared that because of their unbelief which was manifested in their evil confession none of the 10 and none of those who agreed with them would go into the promise land as He had planned. Instead they would die in the desert. Only Joshua and Caleb would go into the land of promise.

> *Numbers 14:28-31 "Say to them, 'As I live,' says the LORD, 'just as you have spoken in My hearing, so I will surely do*

to you; your corpses shall fall in this wilderness, even all your numbered men, according to your complete number from twenty years old and upward, who have grumbled against Me. 'Surely you shall not come into the land in which I swore to settle you, except Caleb the son of Jephunneh and Joshua the son of Nun.

You can see from this situation described in the Old Testament that the faith filled confession of your mouth is very important to your victory and success. When Jesus walked in this kind of authority the "church attendees" of His day said, "what new doctrine is this?"

Some were amazed and followed Him. But many of them were not pleased and thought "who does he think he is"? It was the religious who persecuted Jesus and eventually crucified Him.

However, to their astonishment Jesus said that walking in divine authority is a sure sign that the Kingdom of God has come to the earth. And when He taught the disciples how to pray, getting the kingdom to manifest on earth was the theme.

Jesus said, "if I cast out demons then the

Kingdom of God has come unto you."
Luke 11:20

PRAYER TOOLS PRODUCE SPECIFIC RESULTS

A s tools have different uses and each tool has a design that corresponds to the use, likewise there are different kinds of prayers. So let's think of the different kinds of prayers as tools in our spiritual tool chest. Tools that we will use, pairing up the need to the proper tool to accomplish the task.

James 5:16 The effectual fervent prayer of a righteous man availeth much. (KJV)

Now I've mentioned "spiritual warfare" but don't get nervous.

> *This book is not so much about casting out demons as it is about getting results in prayer, success in your "calling" and thus being fruitful because of the Word of God.*

You and I must seriously ask ourselves, "Are we getting results in our prayers?" If you might acknowledge, that for the most part, you are getting little or no miraculous results from your prayers you will gain much from this book. For to deny the power of results from the Gospel is to be left with just a form of religion. Most of Christendom is currently content with a form of religion, devoid of true supernatural power.

> *II Timothy 3:5 ...holding to a form of godliness, although they have denied its power; and avoid such men as these.*

The subject of our book is prayer, but a specific type of prayer. There are different kinds of prayer, all of which are valid and have their place. The following are used as an example of the various categories of prayer.

They are:

- Prayers of Confession

- Prayers of Repentance
- Prayers of Praise and thanksgiving
- Prayers of Petition and supplication
- Prayers of Pardon
- Prayers of Protection
- Prayers of Intercession

CONFESSION

Confession is a useful tool when we have sinned, disobeyed or disappointed the Holy Spirit.

John speaks of this all-important aspect as being useful to keep our relationship with God open and flowing freely in I John 1:9.

I John 1:9 If we confess our sins, He is faithful and righteous to forgive us our sins and to cleanse us from all unrighteousness.

REPENTANCE

Repentance is a useful tool when we have sinned, disobeyed and we want to correct our behavior for the future. Repentance sets us upon the right path toward God and notifies the devil of our changed mind.

> *Acts 2:38 And Peter said to them, "Repent, and let each of you be baptized in the name of Jesus Christ for the forgiveness of your sins; and you shall receive the gift of the Holy Spirit..."*

> *Acts 3:19,20 "Repent therefore and return, that your sins may be wiped away, in order that times of refreshing may come from the presence of the Lord; and that He may send Jesus, the Christ appointed for you..."*

PRAISE AND THANKSGIVING

Praise & thanksgiving is a useful tool when we approach God, commune with God, honor Him, worship Him, reflect upon God's goodness or when we have prayed and we believe that God has heard us and the answer is forthcoming.

*Psalm 100:4 Enter His gates with
thanksgiving, And His courts with praise.
Give thanks to Him; bless His name.*

PETITION AND SUPPLICATION

Petition & supplication are useful tools when we have a request of the Father.   When we don't' know his will, we will petition Him. When we have a request of Him that only He can fulfill then we ask of Him. When we have a burden to lay at His feet then we bring this to him in supplication.

Paul speaks of this prayer tool in Philippians 4.

*Philippians 4:6 Be anxious for nothing,
but in everything by prayer and
supplication with thanksgiving let your
requests be made known to God.*

PARDON

Pardon is a useful tool when we need the forgiveness that comes through the applied blood of Jesus Christ.

Psalm 51: 1-7 ...be gracious to me, O God, according to Thy lovingkindness; According to the greatness of Thy compassion blot out my transgressions. Wash me thoroughly from my iniquity, And cleanse me from my sin. For I know my transgressions, and my sin is ever before me. Against Thee, thee only, I have sinned, and done what is evil in Thy sight, So that Thou art justified when Thou dost speak, And blameless when Thou dost judge. Behold, I was brought forth in iniquity, and in sin my mother conceived me. Behold, thou dost desire truth in the innermost being, And in the hidden part Thou wilt make me know wisdom. Purify me with hyssop, and I shall be clean; Wash me, and I shall be whiter than snow.

PROTECTION

Protection is a useful tool when we call upon God to remember the covenant and act upon it by keeping us safe or from harm. Psalms 91 is a great example of a prayer of protection.

> *Psalm 91:1-7 He who dwells in the shelter of the Most High Will abide in the shadow of the Almighty. I will say to the LORD, "My refuge and my fortress, My God, in whom I trust!" For it is He who delivers you from the snare of the trapper, And from the deadly pestilence. He will cover you with His pinions, and under His wings you may seek refuge; His faithfulness is a shield and bulwark. You will not be afraid of the terror by night, Or of the arrow that flies by day; Of the pestilence that stalks in darkness, Or of the destruction that lays waste at noon. A thousand may fall at your side, and ten thousand at your right hand; But it shall not approach you.*

INTERCESSION

Intercession is a useful tool when we pray for God to touch others.

> *Ezekiel 22: 30 "And I searched for a man among them who should build up the wall and stand in the gap before Me for the land, that I should not destroy it..."*

There is great power when we get involved in asking God to move on behalf of others. He loves this kind of partnership in the earth and depends upon us taking on this role as ministers of reconciliation. Paul wept over His converts and the Cities he was called to.

> *Galatians 4: 19 My children, with whom I am again in labor until Christ is formed in you—*

Here we've listed seven different types of prayer and there are still others, each one being like a different tool.

I want to illustrate the effectiveness of each type of prayer that I've just described by asking you think about all the tools a man might have stored away for projects in his garage. Each tool has a different function and usefulness.

For instance, a skill saw might be kept on hand to cut boards. This tool would be better for cutting boards than a **hand plane...or a power plane, a hammer for drill.**

A shovel might be kept on hand for digging up certain items around the yard or transporting small quantities of dirt. A shovel would be better for this purpose than a fertilizer machine or drop light.

As tools have different uses and each tool has a design that corresponds to the use, likewise there are different kinds of prayers. So let's think of the different kinds of prayers as tools in our spiritual tool chest. Tools that we will use, pairing up the need to the proper tool to accomplish the task. Now let's look at a radical tool that God has given us that corresponds with the granting of His authority.

ONE PRAYER TOOL STANDS OUT

We've wrongfully lumped all spiritual communication into one realm. That's why when someone speaks with boldness into the spirit realm someone says they're trying to boss God around. We need to recapture the power of speaking for God.

One of the most important kinds of prayer (and our topic for this book) does not really look like prayer at all...and that might one of the reasons we overlook it and don't use it like we should. What does prayer look like?

Most of us have formed a "spiritual" or "religious" perspective on what we think prayer is. Much of this is based simply on our exposure to prayer. Most all of the prayer tools that we normally use are **talking with God in design**.... Much the way you would talk with an employer or a parent.

The **petition** tool might look like this... "Dear Father, could you help us buy a new car real soon."

The **confession** tool might look like this..."Father I admit that I am in need of your wisdom with my children." Or "Father, I admit that I have been running from you and you're leading." Or, "Father, I sinned today when I talked to my wife in a harsh manner..."

The **repentance** tool might look like this..."Father, I see what you want me to do now and I repent from my selfishness, I will follow you and obey your leading from now on. I turn my back on anger and selfishness. I am done with those behaviors and feelings. "You'll notice with almost all of the tools of prayer that we are the most familiar with, they all involve a dialogue with God and often the requesting of something from God.

These kinds of prayers have become so ingrained into the **prayer perspective** of <u>Christians that they have failed to see another type of spiritual activity that belongs in the prayer category</u>.

Since we have the idea that all prayer looks alike, we have inadvertently missed an important prayer tool that looks altogether different.

> *The tool that we have forgotten about and the tool that amazed the religious of Jesus' day is the prophetic prayer tool...........*

It could also be called the prayer tool of **proclamation**, the tool of **command**, the tool of **faith**, and the tool of **rebuke**.

Though different synonyms might help describe its function in essence it is the use of **authority**.   It is as Jesus declared mountain moving prayer!

Mark 11:23 "Truly I say to you, whoever

says to this mountain, 'Be taken up and
cast into the sea,' and does not doubt in
his heart, but believes that what he says is
going to happen, it shall be granted him.

When Jesus used this tool the religious said, "what **authority**, even the demons obey Him..." Jesus used this tool when He stood in His authority as the son of God and commanded things to happen; bodies to be healed and demons to depart.

Mark 1:27 And they were all amazed, so
that they debated among themselves,
saying, "What is this? A new teaching with
authority! He commands even the unclean
spirits, and they obey Him."

Carlos Annacondia is a man whose life embodies this principle of commanding. He has been at the forefront of a revival in Argentina for some years. According to C. Peter Wagner, "when he shouts "Listen to me Satan" demons manifest and the demonized victims are taken out and ministered to one-on-one (from the foreword of Satan Listen to me).

Here's the description of his book "Satan Listen to me" from Christianbook.com.

According to this Argentinian evangelist, it's time for believers to take control of the works of the devil and his demons. He believes that with the right instruction, readers can gain access to the supernatural powers of the Holy Spirit, avoid Satan's snares, and cast out demons.

> *The Church has forgotten this tool of commanding to the point that few ever pray with the same authority that Jesus prayed with.*

We've become like the religious observers of His day. If someone were to come into our midst and pray with authority like Jesus, we would be flabbergasted and say, "what new doctrine is this, they act like they are hot stuff, who do they think they are..."

We've forgotten and forsaken the power of commanding things to change, spirits to depart, sickness to go and mountains to move.

In it's place we've substituted other tools, tools that are far less effective for the purpose necessary. For these prayers of mountain moving **authority** we've substituted prayers of **petition, pardon, protection and supplication and intercession**.

Don't get me wrong, these other prayer tools are right and good in the right place, but using the wrong prayer is worse than using a tool to do a job it was not created to do.

Let's take and consider some examples in the natural realm. Have you tried to "rip" plywood into smaller strips of wood with a drill? Plywood comes in sheets of 4' x 8'. Many times the use of plywood requires cutting or "ripping" it down in to thinner strips. Imagine doing this with a drill. Wouldn't that be exasperating?

Imagine cutting a 4 X 8 sheet of plywood with a drill.

- You first set the wood up on the saw horses.
- You mark the size of the cut that you want to accomplish.
- You snap a chalk line on the wood so you know exactly where you are going to cut.
- You proceed to take a drill with a ¼ inch bit and start drilling holes down the chalk line.

Twenty minutes later you are still in the garage and nearly half way done. In my case my wife would come out and check my temperature, because she would figure I've lost my mind. Why, because setting on the shelf in the garage is a perfect good skill saw designed for accomplishing that cut in 45 seconds.

How about some other mis-uses of tools...?

Have you tried to drill a hole with a handsaw?

Have you tried to cut a board with a hand plane?

Don't get me wrong, each of these afore mentioned tools are good tools, but some negative effect takes place when you try to accomplish a task with the wrong tool.

THE SIMPLE SOLUTION TO UNANSWERED PRAYER

The sincere believer is working up a sweat but using the wrong tool. Sincerity is not the prerequisite to answered prayer and neither is effort or need. God is a person of creative order and all that He has ordained is by purpose.

Three things happen when Christians use the wrong spiritual tool to bring about a desired (or promised) result.

1. The user of the tool looks foolish and ineffective.

2. The tool looks poorly designed, foolish and ineffective.

3. The manufacturer of the tool looks foolish and out of touch with the needs of the user. The above three scenarios have been played out time and time again as it pertains to Christianity, God and prayer.

> *Christians often look foolish and ineffective because their prayers are not working.*

How many times have your "prayers" not been "answered"? Most Christians have no idea if their prayers will get answered.

This is one of the reasons why we don't pray for people with boldness. This "unknown" affects how we engage with the unsaved. We don't know how to get answers from heaven, so we aren't able to show off the power of God with confidence. Think about how bold you'd be if you knew you could affect a change when you pray.

Some years ago, one of our church members called me up to ask if I'd go to the hospital and pray for his employer's son. The family didn't really know the Lord, but their son was in critical condition at the hospital. This little five-year-old was playing outside and accidently run over by his mother in their Ford Excursion as she was backing out of the garage. A Ford Excursion is the largest SUV Ford Motor Company has made. It's a 7000 lb. vehicle and the rear tire had run over his chest. Now he lay in the hospital paralyzed from the neck down. I grieved for the pain of the parents, and I jumped at the opportunity.

This was a chance to bring God's power to bear against a terrible situation. When I arrived I introduced myself and exchanged some pleasantries.

The father was present and wanted to be in the room when I prayed. Therefore, I felt a need to explain to him that I would not be praying for his son like he might have understood prayer. I was going to command the boy to be restored and he would be restored.

I asked him to work with me by speaking restoration over the boy himself in the coming days and weeks. Once he understood what I was saying I did my part. I would admit I didn't have any flash of lightning come in the room, not jolt of power, but God moved, and it came to pass as I had said it would. Quickly the boy began to recover and regain feeling and movement.

How many times have you stepped out in faith and made a petition to God when you were supposed to command Lazarus to come forth?

Have you experienced this?

How many times?

How has it affected you?

Doesn't it make you hesitant to pray again in the future?

> *Prayer is slandered, thought dumb, dishonored and assumed to be out of date and or a foolish thing that the superstitious did years ago.*

Have you are struggled with this feeling?

Have you fully overcome this?

Do you see this tendency in our post–Christian culture?

> *God looks out of touch and uncaring because it appears that He doesn't answer very many of these "prayers" that He told people to pray.*

Do you feel this way sometimes?

How do you rationalize this and explain it to people?

A common cry of people is "where is God anyway?" "If God cared He'd help me!"

People don't understand a God that is so distant and uninvolved with their needs.

It's no wonder that people aren't being attracted to the God that we profess. They usually figure that <u>they can do better on their own</u>. And many times, it appears that they can.

The truth is we are often only able to offer "spiritual" salvation and the hope of eternal life to those who have tangible needs.

This problem, as I've explained it, explains one of the major reasons why often the Christian fails to receive the answer to his/her prayer. He is praying, and he is praying hard and fast. He is praying long. He is sincere, he is praying from a pure heart, but all the while nothing is happening.

Why? He is trying to cut a board with a drill instead of a skill saw.

The sincere believer is working up a sweat but using the wrong tool. Sincerity is not the prerequisite to answered prayer and neither is your exhausting effort or your deep-seated need.

God is a person of creative order and all that He has ordained is by purpose.

QUENCHING STORMS

*He rose up and confronted the storm
and then spoke to it and commanded
peace and calm to come.*

He knows there are going to be some storms that come up
and some things that rock the boat. But he's not worried
because He is there with you and will confirm His Word with
signs and wonders if necessary.

Removing a storm will serve as another example to using the type of prayer I'm referring to. This and other examples will help us see this kind of prayer is used in more than just the casting out of demons. You have authority over nature as well. Mark records the incident.

> Mark 4:35-41 On the same day, when evening had come, He said to them, "**Let us cross over to the other side.**" Now when they had left the multitude, they took Him along in the boat as He was. And other little boats were also with Him. And a great windstorm arose, and the waves beat into the boat, so that it was already filling. But He was in the stern, asleep on a pillow. And they awoke Him and said to Him, "Teacher, do You not care that we are perishing?" **Then He arose and rebuked the wind, and said to the sea, "Peace, be still!"** And the wind ceased and there was a great calm. But He said to them, "Why are you so fearful? How is it that you have no faith?" And they feared exceedingly, and said to one another, "Who can this be, that even the wind and the sea obey Him!"

You note first of all that Jesus announces a destination... *"let us cross over to the other side."*

This is the first key to understanding how to deal with storms, knowing what Jesus has said about the destination. Some storms are in direct violation of the destination.

Some storms are storms we are to confront because they hinder the plan of God, they contradict the destination that God has planned and announced.

Do you see here how Jesus deals with the storm? Remember this was Jesus the man, not Jesus as God. It says that He rose up and confronted the storm and then spoke to it and commanded peace and calm to come.

How do you deal with the storms in your life?

Don't you know that the wind and the sea are to obey you too!

Have you ever wasted time moaning and crying?

Do you look for others who you can tell about how great the storm is?

Do you worry and become filled with fear as you imagine the worst?

Do you focus on the storm and how bad it is?

In a metaphor this story could illustrate your struggles in life; the stormy water in your circumstances, the destination of your destiny, all the while Jesus is in our boat.

What do I mean that Jesus is in your boat? I mean that you are in covenant with God through Him.

He ever lives to help you and represent you before the Father, as a true son and joint heir with Him.

> *Hebrews 7: 25 Hence, also, He is able to save forever those who draw near to God through Him, since He always lives to make intercession for them.*

You are covered with His righteousness.

> *II Corinthians 5:21 He made Him who knew no sin to be sin on our behalf, that we might become the righteousness of God in Him.*

He'll never leave you or forsake you.

> *Hebrews 13: 5 Let your character be free from the love of money, being content with what you have; for He Himself has*

*said, "I WILL NEVER DESERT YOU, NOR
WILL I EVER FORSAKE YOU," 6 so that we
confidently say, "THE LORD IS MY
HELPER, I WILL NOT BE AFRAID. WHAT
SHALL MAN DO TO ME?"*

Through Him you've been made an heir of God and God's Kingdom.

*Romans 8: 16,17 The Spirit Himself bears
witness with our spirit that we are
children of God, and if children, heirs also,
heirs of God and fellow heirs with Christ...*

Through Jesus, the same power, privilege and inheritance that belongs to Him is yours too.

*Ephesians 1:5 He predestined us to
adoption as sons through Jesus Christ to
Himself, according to the kind intention of
His will, to the praise of the glory of His
grace, which He freely bestowed on us in
the Beloved. In Him we have redemption
through His blood, the forgiveness of our
trespasses, according to the riches of His
grace...*

God raised Jesus up and gave to Him the name of all authority, above all other names.

Philippians 2: 9-11 Therefore also God highly exalted Him, and bestowed on Him the name which is above every name, that at the name of Jesus EVERY KNEE SHOULD BOW, of those who are in heaven, and on earth, and under the earth, and that every tongue should confess that Jesus Christ is Lord, to the glory of God the Father.

You, the believer, have His power and authority, and He is with you in the midst of your circumstances and needs.

Matthew 16: 19 "I will give you the keys of the kingdom of heaven; and whatever you shall bind on earth shall be bound in heaven, and whatever you shall loose on earth shall be loosed in heaven."

My question is; what are you doing with all this power and authority?

The power and authority of a new creation life, the power of His indwelling presence within and upon your life?

The apostles of Jesus in the first church knew what to do with this authority and life because Jesus let them taste of it in advance. He sent them out two by two and give them authority over sickness and demons.

> *At that time he told them, "Behold, I have given you authority to tread upon serpents and scorpions, and over all the power of the enemy, and nothing shall injure you."*
> *(Luke 10:19)*

Later He told them...

> *Matthew 16:19 "I will give you the keys of the kingdom of heaven; and whatever you shall bind on earth shall be bound in heaven, and whatever you shall loose on earth shall be loosed in heaven."*

When He told them this and later explained it to them (See Luke 24:49) they understood when they received the Holy Spirit after the resurrection the "*I will give you...*" had come to pass (See John 20:20-22).

The **keys** to heaven imply He has given us the ability to unlock the things in heaven that we need, access these things, so that doors will be opened for us to obtain them. This means access to bring the good things of heaven to the earth realm.

We, in Christ, can unlock the love, the hope, the life, the power, the resource, the health of heaven. etc.

Philippians 4:19 And my God shall supply
all your needs according to His riches in
glory in Christ Jesus.

We also have the keys to lock (bind) spiritual doors and activity in the unclean realm, the realms of hatred, fear, poverty, despair, etc. This implies that we are to use the "keys" close doors on evil and demonic activity.

These keys have been granted us by what Jesus did on our behalf and who He has made us to be before our Father.

He has given us His; righteousness, justification, adoption, the promises, a covenant and dominion all through grace by faith. The result is that we have HIS keys. It's His keys we have full access to.

These are the same keys He had and the same keys that God gave King David.

These keys allow us to come into the presence of God and receive help in our time of need.

> *Hebrews 4: 16 Let us therefore draw near*
> *with confidence to the throne of grace,*
> *that we may receive mercy and may find*
> *grace to help in time of need.*

These keys also allow us to be seated with Christ in the presence of God so that we can alter and decree change on the earth just as Jesus did.

> *Psalm 149: 6 Let the high praises of God*
> *be in their mouth, And a two-edged sword*
> *in their hand, 7 To execute vengeance on*
> *the nations, And punishment on the*
> *peoples; 8 To bind their kings with*
> *chains, And their nobles with fetters of*
> *iron; 9 To execute on them the judgment*
> *written; This is an honor for all His godly*
> *ones. Praise the LORD!*

These are the keys for binding and loosing.

> *Matthew 16: 19 "I will give you the keys of*

the kingdom of heaven; and whatever you shall bind on earth shall be bound in heaven, and whatever you shall loose on earth shall be loosed in heaven."

With these keys, doors are open that no man can shut and doors are closed that no man can open.

Isaiah 45:1 Thus says the LORD to Cyrus His anointed, Whom I have taken by the right hand, To subdue nations before him, And to loose the loins of kings; To open doors before him so that gates will not be shut: 2 "I will go before you and make the rough places smooth; I will shatter the doors of bronze, and cut through their iron bars. 3 "And I will give you the treasures of darkness, And hidden wealth of secret places, In order that you may know that it is I, The LORD, the God of Israel, who calls you by your name.

Revelation 3:7 "And to the angel of the church in Philadelphia write: He who is holy, who is true, who has the key of David, who opens and no one will shut, and who shuts and no one opens..."

Now let's go back to this incident, the incident with the storm Jesus said, "Let us go to the other side". Let's move outside the text to our personal application. Let's consider what this statement could mean to us in our personal lives.

It could mean:

From darkness to light
From Egypt to Canaan
From bondage to promise.
From sickness to health.
From Anxiety to Peace.
From poverty to abundance.
From foolishness to wisdom.

Whatever the case it's because He has something good for us;

- He has named a destination!
- He has all confidence you are going to make it!
- He is going with you and in your boat!
- He has foreknowledge of the storms.
- He knows there are going to be some storms that come up and some things that rock the boat. But he's not worried because He is there with you and

will confirm His Word with signs and wonders if necessary.

WHY WE FAIL IN REMOVING THE STORMS OF LIFE

It's very typical to want Jesus to take care of our storm for us. This perspective is not uncommon and so if you've felt that way don't feel bad. We've been trained this way by religion (Just like the Jews of His day). But God has already granted us His Word and the power to change things in the name of Jesus.

Often when a storm comes, we try everything we can in the natural first. I've done it and you've done it, but now let's be done with it.

- We worry and paint the worst picture possible.
- We discuss every angle of the storm.
- We check the forecast with others who are experiencing storms.
- We imagine how bad it can get.
- We bail water so hard and fast we don't have time to pray for listen to the Holy Spirit.
- We paddle as best as we can trying to get away from the storm.
- We move the rudder into a position that steers us away from the storm.
- We start throwing things overboard, but we are still going down.
- We might eat more chocolate or consider other ways to medicate ourselves.
- We might over sleep or over eat and loose healthy routines because of depression over the storm.
- We might attack others around through a short temper because of the storm.

- We go to the medicine cabinet and look for some soothing pills to calm us down.

Finally, when all else has failed we wake up Jesus and begin to complain. Where have You been, don't You see us, don't You care!!!! You might approach your pastor or some spiritual friend and talk to them about how Jesus doesn't care, and you might go into the ole' "where is God in all of this".

It's very typical to want Jesus to take care of our storm for us.

This perspective is not uncommon and so if you've felt that way don't feel bad. We've been trained this way. We want Him to take away our sin desire, solve our problems, heal our bodies, give us more wealth, deliver us from addictions and bad habits, etc. We want Him to heal our communities and fix our nation. All of this is good and noble.

The problem is we come to Him with prayers of petition for problems that are under our authority to change. God has already granted us His Word and the power to change things in the name of Jesus. With regard to prayer and the storms that come into our lives we usually use the wrong tool to deal with them.

To illustrate we will often pray in the following manner.

CONFESSION

With **Confession** about the storm (or the mountain) ...

"Father I'm just coming to you to tell you there's a mighty big storm, and Father I don't know how much longer I can stand in this storm, because it is mighty big. My check book is empty, and my children are sick ...it just seems that it is getting worse and I don't know if I can go on...but I know you know my needs...oh, Father this trusting you is hard."

Chances are that if you'll be honest with yourself you would admit those prayers don't calm the storm. The next day it is still here just as big as ever, so then we'll try another tool. Granted confession can be good if it is followed by a prayer of authority and faith.

PRAISE

We'll **Praise** Him for the storm... (we heard somewhere that this method really worked good for somebody). Remember "in all things give thanks for this the will of God concerning you."

So, we might say something like...

"Father, I thank you for the storms that you see fit to send my way, I praise you for this storm...I thank you that you know right where I am right now, and you're not going to let me fall. I know that this storm is teaching me something and that I will be better for it.". "This must be your will, so I will praise you for it."

After we finish again usually the storm just continues. Most of the time this is the furthest thing from our mind. As with the disciples we usually are afraid in storms and we start to cry out to Jesus.

> *Jesus says, "peace be still."*

If we do that then we would rejoice at the power of God made manifest through our command. Then we would praise God for the storm because it gave opportunity for God to be glorified.

If we stay paralyzed with fear, then we decide to try another tool.

PETITION

With **Petition** about the storm we'll pray...

"Father please deliver me from this storm. Father I've brought this up before you before and I know that you know what's going on, but please help me, and dear Jesus please take away this...storm, this mountain, this demon, this sickness, this poverty and all of my problems. Oh God you are able, so please help me. In Jesus name, amen."

We hope this one will work. We wait but nothing happens. Jesus is frustrated with us as He was those in the boat because our petitioning is out of fear and not faith.

Others are watching us now to see if our God will deliver. We don't know what to do. A friend tells us that we have hidden sin in our life and that is hindering our answer.

PARDON

Finally, we decide to try a prayer of pardon.

With **Pardon** prayers we'll pray...

"Oh, Father forgive me for causing this storm. Forgive me for whatever I've done to cause this storm. Whatever sin I committed I will repent. I turn away from all my sins, sins of omission and commission. I am so unworthy. No wonder you've allowed this to happen to me. This storm is my fault and I will obey you. Please forgive me, I'm so unworthy."

We wait, thinking this will do it. We are sure of victory now and we feel so clean, but after a few days and weeks we are still struggling with the same old thing. It's true that at times we need to pray a prayer of pardon and forgiveness before a rebuke.

Sometimes we bring storms on to ourselves through sin or disobedience. Mostly we don't' know to pray a prayer of rebuke with authority, so we figure that we are just not being protected from evil. We've not been including this in our prayers lately.

PROTECTION

For **Protection** we'll pray...

"Oh, Father don't let me die with this storm, don't let me go under, please see my situation and rescue me, protect me please from this storm. Don't forget your servant and please help me. Come take this from me and be my help."

I want to suggest usually these prayer tools I've described are the wrong tools for the job.

Generally, none of these tools alone will work to remove the **storms** in your life. Nor will these methods remove the **mountains** in your life, for Jesus told us how to remove mountains in Mark just as he showed us how to remove storms.

> Mark 11: 22 And Jesus answered saying to them, "Have faith in God. "Truly I say to you, **whoever says to this mountain,** **'Be taken up and cast into the sea,'**

*and does not doubt in his heart, but
believes that what he says is going to
happen, it shall be granted him.
"Therefore, I say to you, all things for
which you pray and ask, believe that you
have received them, and they shall be
granted you.*

I would suggest that these methods of prayer when used in the wrong context, as the wrong spiritual tool, become a method of dead religion.

Church has taught us these methods. Church history has taught us these methods, not the New Testament.

The religious pray this way when faced with problems because they have not been taught that they are seated in heavenly places with Christ and that all of creation is longing for the sons of God to take their rightful place of dominion with righteousness. They have not been taught that everything is under your feet when you are seated in heavenly places with Christ.

THESE TRADITIONAL METHODS FALL SHORT

What would happen if you acted like Jesus? What would happen if you acted like you are justified (just as if you never sinned)? God is waiting for us to act in our authority as those who have been deputized to use the name of His son.

STORMS AND MOUNTAINS ARE UNDER YOUR AUTHORITY

Christ came to return dominion to mankind through salvation. Just as storms and mountains and sickness and demons were under Jesus' authority, they are under yours. God will **back up and stand behind** what you demand – declare - require to be done when you pray according to His will.

For hundreds of years we have interpreted "pray" in a limited scope of meaning. Usually we've interpreted "pray" as "ask" or "petition" or "request".

One of the meanings of this all-important word that is interpreted "pray" in the New Testament is **desire** and other is **require**. Require holds the meaning of **demand**.

*John 15:7 If ye abide in me, and my words abide in you, ye shall **ask** what ye will, and it shall be done unto you. "By this My Father is glorified, that you bear much fruit; so you will be My disciples.*

Ask: defined in the Strong's exhaustive concordance #154. aiteo, ahee-teh'-o; of uncert. der.; to ask (in

gen.):--ask, beg, call for, crave, **desire, require**. Comp.
G4441.

What if we substituted these alternative meanings
into this passage?

> *John 15:7 If ye abide in me, and my words
> abide in you, ye shall **require** what ye
> will, and it shall be done unto you. "By
> this My Father is glorified, that you bear
> much fruit; so you will be My disciples.*

> *John 15:7 If ye abide in me, and my words
> abide in you, ye shall **demand** what ye
> will, and it shall be done unto you. "By
> this My Father is glorified, that you bear
> much fruit; so you will be My disciples.*

> *John 15:7 If ye abide in me, and my words
> abide in you, ye shall **desire** what ye will,
> and it shall be done unto you. "By this My
> Father is glorified, that you bear much
> fruit; so you will be My disciples.*

Notice the difference as you begin to see this passage
in the light of a delegate, a deputy of Jesus in the earth.

<u>Consider an illustration of desiring and requiring something to be done.</u>

Let's use your place of employment as the illustration. Let's say that you are a supervisor at a local factory. There is one activity that you might do for the employer, that should you omit this one activity you might as well forget about all the other activities. It is acting on his behalf with those under your charge and working with you.

Let's say that you've been given delegated authority by your employer to make sure something goes the way he wants it. The only way it will go that way is if you use the authority he's given you. In this case you will have to **command....order....demand....require** that something be done in a certain order.

This is the case for us. God has given us His desire, His will, His assignment. In the "Lords prayer" and elsewhere throughout the scripture He said to pray in such a way that the will of God and the Kingdom of God come on earth **exactly as it is in heaven**. This is exactly what Jesus did.

Matthew 12: 28 "But if I cast out demons

*by the Spirit of God, then the kingdom of
God has come upon you."*

This assignment to import the will of God and the Kingdom of God is the "bosses" assignment. If we are not passionate about that assignment, we have missed the purpose of Jesus and the desire God has to restore the earth into a place of His glory, as Isaiah describes.

This is a part of being a Christian that we've forgotten to practice. And because we've failed to practice it we have settled for religious results instead of Kingdom results. We have allowed demons and powers and princes of evil to rule over us, our land, our leadership, our schools, our entertainment industry and commerce instead of casting them out.

Did Jesus demand things to be done? Emphatically, Yes. Did He say we would do greater things than He? Emphatically, Yes. If I am like Christ and demanding, commanding and requiring demon intruders is what He did than I must act like Him.

You might protest and say, "Yes but, that was Him." And "He was God." Yes, that was Him, but he was acting in the power He possessed as a righteous son, not as the divine. That's why He said "it will obey you..." the ordinary disciple of Christ.

> *Luke 17: 6 And the Lord said, "If you had faith like a mustard seed, **you would say** to this mulberry tree, 'Be uprooted and be planted in the sea'; **and it would obey you.***

I fear that Christendom is failing to teach us that we have authority and a responsibility to speak to our storms and mountains. Instead we are content accept them and quake in fear or to ask God to remove them.

I believe God is waiting for us to act in our authority as those who have been deputized to use the name of His son. Consider another illustration, this one of a deputy sheriff.

What would happen to a deputy sheriff in your county if he did not stand in the authority delegated to him by the sheriff and the law? One thing is for sure, he wouldn't have a job very long. Let's say he is called upon for an eviction, but when he arrives at the home of the trespasser stalls and ponders what to do.

He ponders what the sheriff would want done, then eventually he calls the county sheriff and insists that he come and make the eviction for him.

Now this might sound silly, but this is what Christians are doing every day. Imagine if this scenario were happening all across your county? The sheriff would have to go everywhere and show up personally with every case of lawlessness.

- Could the sheriff even stay up?
- Would a system like that work? No!
- How long would that deputy have a job? Not long!

How much work would that deputy get done? Nothing on his own. There would be no use for the deputy if the sheriff has to show up with each and every incident. We know this hypothetical scenario is not the way law enforcement works. So let's learn something from this absurd example. In the natural order of life, we find a picture of spiritual order. So, if things don't make sense in the natural, they won't make sense in the spiritual realm either.

First off, the Sheriff of a county is voted in to his office by the people of that particular county to enforce the law. He is the highest law enforcement agent of the county. Deputies operate under the delegated authority of the sheriff. Deputies act in the place of the stead of the sheriff. They wear the clothing of the sheriff, carry the badge and the gun of the sheriff. He, the deputy, has been delegated all the authority of the State and the County to enforce the legal written code on behalf of the sheriff. When it's his shift and he comes to work, he goes out on assignment, against evil, perpetrators, drunks, abusers, thieves, etc. When he comes up on the scene of wrong doing, he refers to the code and then enforces the law by force if necessary.

The deputy sheriff doesn't consider calling the sheriff, except to get wisdom and knowledge concerning the code. Once he understands the code, he goes to work to enforce it. This is his role as he brings the kingdom of his county and the will of his county into the county just as it is at the County Court House. This deputy sheriff illustration offers a good insight into how we are to live as deputies of sheriff Jesus.

GOD DID NOT SEND THE STORM

God is into storm removal not storm creation. If He is creating storms it is for His enemies, not His covenant friends. God is trying to get peace and blessing into the earth and unto mankind. He is not the source of storms. Every good and perfect gift comes down from God. Storms come because of one of three reasons.

Something wrong with us and our thinking, behavior or methods.

If you are walking in prolonged and willful sin or foolishness, then you bring a storm on yourself. Some storms come because of your own mistakes and sins that allow the enemy or the curse to steal from us.

In that case...

"Submit to God (God's word and way),
resist the devil and he will flee from you."
(James 4:7)

Something in the sphere of influence and authority where He called us. Such as in your City, your denomination or your Church.

God has given you a certain place of authority in your family, in your City, in your Church and in your job, etc. Storms might have been raging before you came along, or they might have started after you came.

Either way God wants you to get the "Word of Wisdom" on the situation from Him and from seeking Him and then speak to the storm. (I John 5:4)

Just as with our City, the storms and spiritual mountains were here before we got here. To obey God, we had to engage the storms and mountains.

It wasn't our fault, but it affected our lives anyway!

- What's affecting you that you inherited?
- What's affecting you that was there before you got there?
- How are you changing it?
- Are you letting it wear you down?

Something as a result of the curse.

STORMS ARE GOING TO COME

Storms will come and they will test the strength of the house you've been building.

> *Matthew 7:24-27 "Therefore everyone who hears these words of Mine, and acts upon them, may be compared to a wise man, who built his house upon the rock. "And the rain descended, and the floods came, and the winds blew, and burst against that house; and yet it did not fall, for it had been founded upon the rock. "And everyone who hears these words of Mine, and does not act upon them, will be like a foolish man, who built his house upon the sand. "And the rain descended, and the floods came, and the winds blew, and burst against that house; and it fell, and great was its fall."*

All the earth is under a curse and you will have to contend with its effects upon you.

The Bible says to "fight the good fight of faith." Blame the devil and blame Adam, but don't blame God. Adam gave us this current situation and through Christ it is a place where your light can shine.

A lot of people can't figure out why all the evil transpires in the world if God is so good. It's because of the curse. This whole earth is under the influence of Satan and under a curse. We have the answer to reverse the curse, but not by just singing a hymn in a building with a steeple.

We need to lay our hands-on maps and command changes to transpire in specific locations with specific people and systems.

We need to go to the City and County buildings, anoint the property with oil and command things to change.

City buildings will be filled with Christian employees and godliness will be on the increase! The removing of storms caused by the curse will bring glory to God.

Romans 5:17 For if by the transgression of the one, death reigned through the one, much more those who receive the abundance of grace and of the gift of righteousness will reign in life through the One, Jesus Christ.

GOD IS NOT STANDING BETWEEN YOU AND THE REMOVAL OF THE STORM

Most Christians are praying as if they must convince God that it would be good if He took away the storm or mountain.

They are praying that way because that is what they define as fervent prayer. They feel that if they can convince Him that it would be good to take away the storm, then they will get their answer. Others feel God sent the storm (in their theology He is sovereign and in control of all things – no room for devils or the curse).

Others feel they probably deserve the storm because they are so unworthy (they will certainly learn a good lesson from this spanking). Many Christians while at the same time with prayer they are trying to convince Him to take away a storm or move a mountain, aren't really sure if He will.

Therefore, about their storms, they pray, "oh God, please remove this storm, if it be thy will." This has a religious and a "submissive" ring to it, but it is misplaced humility. It is always God's will to remove storms and mountains in your life, though at times we may have to discern if we were the ones who put the storm or mountain there due to our own foolishness.

Even in those cases God will remove the mountain or storm when we combine faith with repentance and wisdom.

The "If it be thy will" prayer is more often meant to be a prayer for guidance, discernment combined with submission. It's best to pray that way when you need to discern God's purpose and will.

Let's say you have an idea or a direction, but you don't know if it's God's highest and best direction, you have sought Him, but not heard yet, then you might pray...

Grant me this job, "if it be thy will."

Give us a boy, "if it be thy will."

Give us the purchase of this home, "if it be thy will."

In this way you are submitting the outcome to God, you are trusting Him because you really don't have His Word on the matter. This is a fine use of "if it be thy will" prayer.

It is also useful as a clarification to submitting to God's will when you already know what God's will is. Jesus prayed that prayer in the garden. It was appropriate as He knelt before the Father in a time of submission and sacrifice.

> *Matthew 26: 39 And He went a little beyond them, and fell on His face and prayed, saying, "My Father, if it is possible, let this cup pass from Me; <u>yet not as I will, but as Thou wilt."</u>*

"If it be thy will" would have been the wrong way for Ezekiel to pray when God had already said to Him, "command these bones to live".

Initially Ezekiel didn't know God's will, so he replies, "O Lord God, Thou knowest."

> *Ezekiel 37: 37:1 The hand of the LORD was upon me, and He brought me out by the Spirit of the LORD and set me down in the middle of the valley; and it was full of bones.*
>
> *2 And He caused me to pass among them round about, and behold, there were very many on the surface of the valley; and lo, they were very dry. 3 And He said to me, "Son of man, can these bones live?" And I answered, "O Lord GOD, Thou knowest."*

But then in verse 4 God told him His will.

Ezekiel 37: 4 Again He said to me,
"Prophesy over these bones, and say to
them, 'O dry bones, hear the word of the
LORD.' 5 "Thus says the Lord GOD to
these bones, 'Behold, I will cause breath to
enter you that you may come to life.

When God reveals His will, it becomes inappropriate from that moment forward to use an "if it be thy will" prayer - nor is it a true act of faith. It would not have been appropriate for Jesus to have cursed the fig tree with a "if it be thy will" curse. You'll see this as recorded by Mark.

Mark 11: 13 And seeing at a distance a fig
tree in leaf, He went to see if perhaps He
would find anything on it; and when He
came to it, He found nothing but leaves,
for it was not the season for figs. 14 And
He answered and said to it, "May no one
ever eat fruit from you again!"

Can you imagine Him adding, "if it be thy will?" He already knew God's will concerning the fig tree as He had already heard from God in His spirit. That's why when they questioned Him, He said, *"have faith in God."* (Mark 11:22) We need to shed the wondering if God wants storms and mountains out of our lives.

> *You really have to ask, if you don't think it is God's will to move the mountains out of your life, <u>why do you work so hard in the natural to move them</u>.*

Aren't you then resisting God? God is not trying to get more storms and mountains into your world, He sent Jesus to defeat the power of storms and mountains. It's strange how we in religion say we don't know God's will on healing, but we rush off to the doctor to get medicine to get well.

> *I John 3:8 ...The Son of God appeared for this purpose, that He might destroy the works of the devil.*

It is always God's will to help us and better our lives. Why would He go to all the trouble to save us by the death of His Son just to see us grovel in the curse and destruction.

In Romans 8:32　Paul says it so well:

"He who did not spare His own Son, but delivered Him up for us all, how will He not also with Him freely give us all things?"

I think we just don't know how to get the healing result that is promised to us, so we play it safe by saying "if it be thy will". So many have failed in their healing prayers that we have no confidence to pray with boldness, thinking we might fail too. And fail we may if we continue in these prayers that lack authority. Note that I'm talking to born again Christians who are following Jesus with all their heart and strength. If a Christian has prolonged-willful sin in their lives this introduces a different issue. In this case they have invited a storm and they are fortifying a mountain of resistance due to their lack of repentance.

James 4:6 ...Therefore it says, "GOD IS OPPOSED TO THE PROUD, BUT GIVES GRACE TO THE HUMBLE."

Another problem that feeds dysfunctional faith; Religion will teach you that storms and mountains (obstacles, problems, difficulties and trials) are the <u>only way</u> that God can teach you, that you need these things so that you will grow and mature.

If you believe this, you will think that storms are God's will. If they are God's will and he is using them to perfect you then you will not have confidence to resist them. This teaching is a contradiction to the Word.

The Word declares that we grow and are equipped through the <u>leaders in our lives</u>, through the <u>Word of God</u> and through the <u>leading of the Holy Spirit</u>. These three agencies are the teachers.

Ephesians 4: 11 And He gave some as apostles, and some as prophets, and some as evangelists, and some as pastors and teachers, 12 for the equipping of the saints for the work of service, to the building up of the body of Christ; 13 until we all attain to the unity of the faith...

2 Timothy 3: 16 All Scripture is inspired by God and profitable for teaching, for reproof, for correction, for training in righteousness; 17 that the man of God may be adequate, equipped for every good work.

Romans 8: 14 For all who are being led by the Spirit of God, these are sons of God.

If we are willingly rebellious then our circumstances will go sour. But even then it doesn't mean we have grown. We are just a person with sour circumstances. Only when we turn to the three sources of wisdom do we grow.

So, if in the midst of sour circumstances, we humble ourselves and turn to God we can grow. It's not necessarily true when people say, they <u>had</u> to go through something. It could be that they refused to listen and change and humble themselves under the sources of wisdom, therefore they had to go through something.

GOD WILL BACK UP YOUR FAITH WITH MIRACLES

John 15:7 If ye abide in me, and my words abide in you, ye shall ask what ye will, and it shall be done unto you. "By this My Father is glorified, that you bear much fruit; so you will be My disciples..."

We lack the confidence that comes with faith because we often lack the Word that brings faith. Determining

God's will is definitely the key to successful prayer, but most of God's will for mankind is revealed in the scriptures.   If we come into a situation where His will is not known, then is the responsibility as an ambassador to seek God until we know His will.

> *Jeremiah 33: 3 'Call to Me, and I will answer you, and I will tell you great and mighty things, which you do not know.'*

It is not appropriate to pray a prayer that "leaves it up to God" and thus continue to walk on without understanding, yet this is what most Christians do. This isn't blind faith, this is being blind. Faith is based on a knowing that comes from God.

> *Romans 10: 17 So then faith cometh by hearing, and hearing by the word of God (KJV).*

God doesn't want to come down and assert His will and leave you, His ambassador, out of the picture.

You aren't a puppet. You are a son. You must concern yourself with God's will.

Once you know God's will for a situation you know what to stand for and how to posture your faith and confession. You represent God and His will in the earth just as Jesus did.

Jesus did not live one day of His ministry without ascertaining the knowledge of the Fathers will. If he lacked knowledge, He spent time in prayer until He had the knowing.

Armed with the answers He acted just as God would have. That's why He said, "if you've seen me, you've seen the Father." That's why He said, "I don't do anything unless I see my Father do it or hear my Father say it."

"Truly, truly, I say to you, the Son can do nothing of Himself, unless it is something He sees the Father doing; for whatever the Father does, these things the Son also does in like manner.

Every morning Jesus got up before it was daylight and went to a lonely place to pray. It was there that He would hear from God. It was there that He would learn of the Fathers will and desires. The result would be faith to act upon the Word of God.

> *Isaiah 50:4,5 The Lord GOD has given Me the tongue of disciples, That I may know how to sustain the weary one with a word. He awakens Me morning by morning, He awakens My ear to listen as a disciple. The Lord GOD has opened My ear; And I was not disobedient, Nor did I turn back.*

Just like He did with Jesus, God will back up the things that you <u>demand</u> and <u>decree</u> in the spirit realm. Imagine yourself working for a contractor. For several years I worked for a mid-sized construction firm. Each morning I would come to the office where the owner would be ready for the day.

Every day he would give me instructions for the work to be performed. I would leave that office and act on his behalf based on the word of his instruction.

You also have been given delegated authority by your Father to make sure something goes the way He wants it and the only way it will go that way is if you use the authority He's given you. In this case you are

commanding....ordering....demanding....that something be done in a certain order.

> *John 15:7 If ye abide in me, and my words abide in you,* ***ye shall ask what ye will,*** *and it shall be done unto you. "By this My Father is glorified, that you bear much fruit; so you will be My disciples..."*

So, we see that through abiding in the Word of God we can understand and discern the will of God, then we can require that it comes into the earth realm. Sometimes interceding and sometimes commanding. I'm going to petition God to show His favor and mercy to the unbelievers in my City, then I'm going to confront and drive out demons and spirits who hinder righteousness.

Now you might be living the fairly good life and enjoying the blessing of God to a good degree, because you've been born again and you've been forgiven and you are on your way to heaven, but I want to ask you...

- Is that all there is to it?
- Is that all that God saved you for?

- Are you seeing the same level of influence and the same works that Jesus saw?

- I'm asking have you come out of bondage just to settle for **mediocrity**?

- Is it enough that you maintain a fairly decent life and make it through to heaven?

Isn't there a land of dominion a land of promise?

Isn't there a place of Glory in God where you begin to rule in life as Christ?

I'm asking you, have you settled for **Good instead of the Best?** If you want the best you have to begin to act like the delegated authority that you are in the earth. The Lord convicted me with Ezekiel 47. He said that I was so excited about being waist deep in the things of God, that I had stopped growing and trusting Him. I had become content and proud. I was proud because I wasn't ankle deep like I used to be. I was content, because I was a experiencing a measure of the Spirit, a measure beyond where I had previously been.

- As it pertains to your mind, you can know what the will of God is.

- As it pertains to sickness and health, you can know what the will of God is.

- As it pertains to your family, you can know what the will of God is.

- As it pertains to your city and community, you can know what the will of God is.

- As it pertains to your church, you can know what the will of God is.

WHERE YOU KNOW THE WILL OF GOD YOU ARE CALLED TO FIGHT FOR IT

Jesus called this binding and loosing...

God with Jeremiah called this plucking and planting...

> *Jeremiah 1:9 Then the LORD stretched out His hand and touched my mouth, and the LORD said to me, "Behold, I have put My words in your mouth. "See, I have appointed you this day over the nations and over the kingdoms, To **pluck up and to break down**, To **destroy and to overthrow**, To **build and to plant**."*

God has given us His word, His will, His knowledge and understanding so that we will take dominion in this world and rule over it in righteousness. Of this assignment He hasn't changed His mind.

> *Genesis 1: 28 And God blessed them, and God said unto them, Be fruitful, and multiply, and replenish the earth, and subdue it: and have **dominion** over the fish of the sea, and over the fowl of the air, and over every living thing that moveth upon the earth. (KJV)*

There is no other tool for establishing His dominion in the earth. His Word and His will is the basis for all government and life.

> *Isaiah 9: 6,7 For a child will be born to us, a son will be given to us; And the government will rest on His shoulders; And His name will be called Wonderful Counselor, Mighty God, Eternal Father, Prince of Peace. There will be no end to the increase of His government or of peace, On the throne of David and over his kingdom, To establish it and to uphold it*

*with justice and righteousness From then
on and forevermore. The zeal of the LORD
of hosts will accomplish this.*

HEAVEN AND EARTH WILL PASS AWAY, BUT NOT HIS WORD.

*Matthew 24: 35 "Heaven and earth will
pass away, but My words shall not pass
away."*

His Word will accomplish what it is sent out to do.

*Isaiah 55: 11 So shall My word be which
goes forth from My mouth; It shall not
return to Me empty, without
accomplishing what I desire, And without
succeeding in the matter for which I sent
it.*

Now we must see that we are the vessels of the sending of the Word of God. We are the tools of His declaration, **just as Jeremiah was.**

He is not using angels in this day to declare His will, His angels in this age are the servants of His Word in our mouth, as it was with Daniel (Hebrews 1:14).

See what the angel said when he came to Daniel...

Daniel 10:12 Then he said to me, "Do not be afraid, Daniel, for from the first day that you set your heart on understanding this and on humbling yourself before your God, your words were heard, and I have come in response to your words.

Jeremiah was a man. He stood in the office of prophet, now look again at what God told Jeremiah that through his words He would accomplish.

PLUCK UP AND BREAKDOWN...

This phrase is an agricultural term. God uses agricultural language to illustrate the way things grow and develop in the earth and in spiritual kingdoms.

DESTROY AND OVERTHROW

This is an architectural metaphor. God uses architectural language to further illustrate the same point. Through these two metaphors He clearly shows us how all things begin, grow and change for new growth whether spiritual or physical.

BUILD AND PLANT

Then using again, the same two metaphors, as throughout all scriptures, He says that with our words we are to build and plant the things we desire and the things He desires.

Thus, He shows us that in many and most cases there are two steps to the making of progress for good.

- Plucking and then planting
- Destroying and building.

God Himself started with something that was needing a change. The earth was formless and dark. This is an example of how you and I must start to bring change to all of life.

Genesis 1:2 Now the earth was formless and empty, darkness was over the surface of the deep, and the Spirit of God was hovering over the waters. And God said, "Let there be light," and there was light.

Hebrews 10: 9 ... He takes away the first in order to establish the second.
Romans 4: 17 ...as it is written, "A FATHER OF MANY NATIONS HAVE I MADE YOU" in the sight of Him whom he believed, even God, who gives life to the dead and calls into being that which does not exist.

It's not uncommon for God to take something away and to establish something better. As we've seen, this is a farming principle too. When you see something evil what are you to do?

Through the prophet Jeremiah God has shown us the pattern in coming against evil.

Confront it with your words, declare it fallen, rebuke it, declare it fallen and overthrown!

Then don't stop there, continue with bold speech, continue to bring forth God's will and plant and

> *build by declaring the good things that God has desired and call them to come forth.*

Call new things into the now. Call them into the present. Call them completed.

JESUS THE VICTORY EXAMPLE TO FOLLOW

Luke 4:38...But Simon's wife's mother was sick with a high fever, and they made request of Him concerning her. So, He stood over her and rebuked the fever, and it left her. And immediately she arose and served them.

Jesus did not ask God to take away this fever "if it be His will", because He already knew the Fathers will concerning *sickness. He had come from the Father to "destroy the works of the devil" in the earth.*

The best way to see how to use this powerful tool of prayer is to look at Jesus. Jesus used the same authority that Jeremiah was instructed to use.

Jesus took it beyond the scope of nations to personalize God's power to the healing of people, casting out of demons and even paying taxes. As His disciples we are to act just as He did. We are to use this tool just as He used it.

JESUS WITH SICKNESS AND DISEASE.

Jesus never prayed for sickness in our current religious tradition. In Mark 5: 35-4 there is record of Jesus healing the daughter of the synagogue official. Mark 5:41,42 Then He took the child by the hand, and said to her, "Talitha, cumi," which is translated, "Little girl, I say to you, arise." Immediately the girl arose and walked, for she was twelve years of age. And they were overcome with great amazement. You'll notice that Jesus told her what to do, (I say to you arise) and with authority believed that everything that was necessary for this to happen would be released as He spoke the command.

Likewise, with Peter's mother in Law. Notice how Matthew relates the story then we'll look at it as written by Doctor Luke. Matthew. 8: 14-17 And when Jesus had come to Peter's home, He saw his mother-in-law lying sick in bed with a fever. And He touched her hand, and the fever left her; and she arose, and waited on Him. And when evening had come, they brought to Him many who were demon-possessed; and He cast out the spirits with a word and healed all who were ill in order that what was spoken through Isaiah the prophet might be fulfilled, saying, "HE HIMSELF TOOK OUR INFIRMITIES, AND CARRIED AWAY OUR DISEASES." NASB.

Luke gives us more insight into what really happened in the room that day when Jesus healed Peter's mother-in-law.

> Luke 4:38...But Simon's wife's mother was
> sick with a high fever, and they made
> request of Him concerning her. So, He

*stood over her **and rebuked the fever**,*
and it left her. And immediately she arose
and served them.

Luke points out that something Jesus did was the key to the healing. Jesus did not just touch this lady, but He also **rebuked the fever** and when He did, the cause of the fever.

He did not ask God to take away the fever "if it be His will", because He already knew the Fathers will concerning sickness. He had come from the Father to "destroy the works of the devil" in the earth. He did not, apparently, cast out a demon this time as was common because there wasn't a demon to be cast out. Fevers are the result of the curse of disobedience as recorded in Deuteronomy 28.

Deut. 28:22 "The LORD will smite you
with consumption and with fever and
with inflammation and with fiery heat
and with the sword and with blight and
with mildew, and they shall pursue you
until you perish."

It was the Father's will that Jesus destroy the works of the curse, the devil and sickness and infirmity. Look back at the passage now as Matthew recorded it. You'll see that Jesus did this to fulfill what the Father had already declared through the mouth of His prophets (Matthew 8:17).

Over and over again throughout the scriptures you'll see the pattern of healing and deliverance was with authority and a command.

> *Mark 1:40 Now a leper came to Him, imploring Him, kneeling down to Him and saying to Him, "If You are willing, You can make me clean." Then Jesus, moved with compassion, stretched out His hand and touched him, and said to him, "I am willing; be cleansed."*

This is now the way God wants us to operate in the earth. We are deputized with His name!

Jesus said greater works shall you do because I go to the Father... but we have not used the proper tool and therefore we have not seen the greater works.

JOHN 14:12 "Most assuredly, I say to you, he who believes in Me, the works that I do he will do also; and greater works than these he will do, because I go to My Father."

JESUS CONQUERS DEMON SPIRITS

Jesus never asked demons to depart, never talked to them nicely, never allowed them to control Him and never did He ask the Father to take them away.

Luke 4:33 Now in the synagogue there was a man who had a spirit of an unclean demon. And he cried out with a loud voice, saying, "Let us alone! What have we to do with You, Jesus of Nazareth? Did You come to destroy us? I know who You are; the Holy One of God!" But Jesus **rebuked him, saying, "Be quiet, and come out of him!"** And when the demon had thrown him in their midst, it came out of him and did not hurt him.

Luke 4:36 Then they were all amazed and

*spoke among themselves, saying, "What a word this is! **For with authority and power He commands** the unclean spirits, and they come out."*

THE APOSTLES - AN
EXAMPLE OF VICTORY

The apostles learned from Jesus. They
learned from the master.

Then they were anointed by the Holy Spirit. Therefore, they too, like Jesus, never prayed for the sick. Certainly, they didn't pray for the sick according to our tradition. Look at Peter and his prayer for the lame man. You won't see this kind of prayer with too many Christians, even in church on a Sunday morning.

Acts 3: 6 But Peter said, "I do not possess silver and gold, but what I do have I give to you: **In the name of Jesus Christ the Nazarene-- walk!"**

Acts 9:32-35 the sick man that Peter spoke to...

Acts 9:33,34 There (in Lydda) he found a certain man named Aeneas, who had been bedridden eight years and was paralyzed. And Peter **said to him, "Aeneas, Jesus the Christ heals you. Arise and make your bed. "** Then he arose immediately.

The apostles never asked God to take away demons. They did not try to counsel them out, they did not call them multiple personalities disorder, ADD, ADHD, blunt trauma, post-traumatic stress syndrome. They confronted the enemies of peace and drove
them out.

Acts 16: 18 And she continued doing this for many days. But Paul was greatly annoyed, and turned and said to the spirit, ***"I command you in the name of Jesus Christ to come out of her!"*** *And it came out at that very moment.*

THE PRAYER OF FAITH
WILL HEAL

I usually thought I had to preach pray...meaning that I would preach a good sermon in my prayer and hopefully work myself and the client into a place of faith.   Most of my praying was more for me than anyone. Through reciting scriptures and some hallelujahs thrown in there I would hopefully get myself headed in the direction of faith.

I hope you are seeing that this commanding and requiring is normative for believers who are deputies of God in the earth.

This kind of prayer is what we should call the **"prayer of faith**."

There is a reference to the "prayer of faith" in the book of James.

James 5:14... And the prayer of faith shall save the sick...

What could James have meant? There has been a lot of discussion and speculation over this issue of the "prayer of faith." James says that if the elders will pray the "prayer of faith" over a sick man he will be raised up.

What is the prayer of Faith?

Have you ever prayed it?

Is it common these days?

James 5:14,15 Is any sick among you? let him call for the elders of the church; and let them pray over him, anointing him with oil in the name of the Lord: And the prayer of faith shall save the sick, and the

*Lord shall raise him up; and if he have
committed sins, they shall be forgiven
him.*

Most of us would say that the prayer of faith is to
"pray with faith." This would seem to be a logical
explanation for what James meant in this passage. In
that case the "prayer of faith" might sound like this.

"Oh God I really **believe** that you heal and so I ask you
to heal this person in Jesus name, heal them now **by
faith**, Amen."

That's how I've prayed the "prayer of faith" for years.
Of course, along with such a prayer I would pray a good
five minutes or more and recite to all the scriptures I
could remember on faith and on healing, thinking if I
didn't probably nothing would happen.

Isn't that the way you've prayed too?

I usually thought (subconsciously) I had to "preach
pray" ...meaning that I would preach a good sermon in
my prayer and hopefully work myself and the client into
a place of faith. Most of my praying was more for me
than anyone. Through reciting scriptures and some

hallelujahs thrown in there I would hopefully get myself headed in the direction of faith.

It could be in all the conjecture of what the "prayer of faith" is we've missed it. I found that usually it is best when interpreting the Bible, to follow two principles of interpretation.

First we should interpret the Bible with the Bible; that is where else is this terminology discussed?

Secondly, we need to look within the context of the text for clues (like parallels or illustrations).

Using the first principle of interpretation means doing a study on "faith" and where "faith" is mentioned specifically <u>with regard to prayer.</u> In such a study you will find that a "faith" <u>prayer</u> is always in direct correlation to **commanding** or **saying** something **with authority**, authority because the person praying had was believing that it would come to pass.

Upon close examination you can see that Jesus modeled the "prayer of faith", the prayer that James spoke of in Chapter five. (James 5:14vs)

Matthew 17: 16 "So I brought him to Your

disciples, but they could not cure him." 17 Then Jesus answered and said, "O _faithless and perverse generation, how long shall I be with you? How long shall I bear with you? Bring him here to Me." 18 And Jesus **rebuked the demon**, and it came out of him; and the child was cured from that very hour. 19 Then the disciples came to Jesus privately and said, "Why could we not cast it out?" 20 So Jesus said to them, "Because of your unbelief; for assuredly, I say to you, if you have _faith as a mustard seed,_ **you will say** to this mountain, 'Move from here to there,' and it will move; and nothing will be impossible for you._

Not only did he model the prayer of faith here in Matthew, he also rebuked the disciples for their lack of faith...evidenced by the fact that they didn't take authority over the demon and cast it out.

Mark 4:35 Then He arose and **rebuked the wind, and said to the sea**, "Peace, be still!" And the wind ceased and there

*was a great calm. But He said to them,
"Why are you so fearful? <u>How is it that you
have no faith?</u>"*

Notice here he spoke to the wind and the sea with His mouth.

*Luke 17:5 And the apostles said to the
Lord, "Increase our faith." 6 So the Lord
said, "If you have <u>faith as a mustard seed,
you can **say**</u> to this mulberry tree, 'Be
pulled up by the roots and be planted in
the sea,' and it would obey you.*

Here in this case Jesus said that faith works like a seed. When you have it, you will and must plant it. Your mouth is the planting machine. Therefore, if you have faith about something, you will say something with your mouth.

*Mark. 11:21b "Rabbi, look! The fig tree
which You cursed has withered away."22
So Jesus answered and said to them,
"Have faith in God. 23 "For assuredly, I
say to you, whoever <u>**says**</u> to this*

mountain, 'Be removed and be cast into
the sea,' *and does not doubt in his heart,*
*but believes that those things he **says** will*
be done, he will have whatever he **says**.
24 "Therefore I say to you, whatever
things you ask (DESIRE) when you pray,
believe that you receive them, and you
will have them.

Here He shows them that when you believe something
in your heart you must also speak a command that
corresponds to your faith.

Matthew 21:19 And when he saw a fig tree
in the way, he came to it, and found
*nothing thereon, but leaves only, **and He***
***said to it**, Let no fruit grow on said unto it*
thee henceforward for ever. And presently
the fig tree withered away. 20 And when
the disciples saw it, they marveled, saying,
how soon is the fig tree withered away. 21
Jesus answered and said unto them, Verily
I say unto you, If ye have faith, and doubt
not, ye shall not only do this which is done
*to the fig tree, but also **if ye shall say***
unto this mountain, Be thou removed, and

be thou cast into the sea; it shall be done.
22 And all things, whatsoever ye shall ask
(say) in prayer, believing, ye shall receive.

Here you see that I've substituted the word "say" for the word ask. We should not assume ask is the correct translation of the Greek word "aiteo " because the context is not ask. The context is what you "say".

Say is a typical translation for this word and in this case a more proper translation.

Using the second rule for understanding scripture we need to look at the context of "the prayer of faith" as James used it. Let's look at the scripture again in light of this. I want us to first look at the King James Version.

James 5:14 Is any sick among you? let him
call for the elders of the church; and let
them pray over him, anointing him with
oil in the name of the Lord: 15 And the
prayer of faith shall save the sick, and the
Lord shall raise him up; and if he have
committed sins, they shall be forgiven
him. 16 Confess your faults one to another,
and pray one for , that ye may be healed.

The effectual fervent prayer of a righteous man availeth much. 17 Elias was a man subject to like passions as we are, and he prayed earnestly that it might not rain: and it rained not on the earth by the space of three years and six months. 18 And he prayed again, and the heaven gave rain, and the earth brought forth her fruit.

You'll see to bring an explanation of what James was talking about he used a story (a parallel) out of the Old Testament, a story that the readers would have been familiar with, or at least they could read and get familiar with.

What did Elijah do when "prayed that it might not rain"? And what did he do when he prayed for the heavens to give rain? Let's look.

I Kings 17:1 And Elijah the Tishbite, who was of the inhabitants of Gilead, said unto Ahab, As the LORD God of Israel liveth, before whom I stand, there shall not be dew nor rain these years, but according to my word. KJV

The only scripture we have about Elijah shutting up the skies is found in I Kings 17.

Here we find one of the first mentions of Elijah as well. He comes on the scene with this announcement that HE is shutting the skies, according to the WORD OF THE LORD, or A WORD FROM THE LORD. In other words, God gave him a word that He, God, wanted the skies shut and He tells Elijah to pronounce this decree in order to shut the skies for a period of years.

Then in chapter 18, some three years later, we see that THE WORD OF THE LORD came to Elijah saying it was time to send rain upon the land.

I Kings 18:1 Now it came about after many days, that the word of the LORD came to Elijah in the third year, saying, "Go, show yourself to Ahab, and I will send rain on the face of the earth." NASB

After a slaughter of the false prophets Elijah goes up on the mountain to call the rain forth. You'll notice that he had so much faith that the rain would be coming that he told Ahab to go eat and drink (as in celebration).

> *I Kings 18:41 And Elijah said unto Ahab, get thee up, eat and drink; for there is a sound of abundance of rain. 42 So Ahab went up to eat and to drink. And Elijah went up to the top of Carmel; and he cast himself down upon the earth, and put his face between his knees, 43 And said to his servant, Go up now, look toward the sea. And he went up, and looked, and said, there is nothing. And he said, <u>Go again seven times</u>. 44 And it came to pass at the seventh time, that he said, Behold, there ariseth a little cloud out of the sea, like a man's hand. And he said, go up, say unto Ahab, Prepare thy chariot, and get thee down, that the rain stop thee not. 45 And it came to pass in the meanwhile, that the heaven was black with clouds and wind, and there was a great rain. KJV*

Maybe you've assumed this was a petition prayer. Kind of a, "God please send the rain!"

Maybe you've never thought about it. I personally think this was a commanding declaration. Think about it. When God announces His will to us and gives us a picture of what He is doing, releasing and about to do, does He need us to petition Him to do it?

Did Jesus petition the Father for the things revealed to Him as the will of Father? No. Could that be a form of unbelief? Ignorance? Poor theological training?

Our traditions making null the Word? Pride and false humility? Depreciation of who we are "in Christ?"

For me it was a mixture of all of the above.

If we look at how our Father has worked in scripture, when He announces His will, He just needs His prophetic delegate to announce it and call it forth. This, that Elijah did, was a type of "whatsoever you bind will be bound, whatsoever you lose will be loosed." Matthew 16:19vsf

When Elijah put his face between his knees, I don't think it was to beg God to do something, but to command clouds to come. You'll see that he continued in this "fervent prayer" seven times. He believes that clouds are gathering and coming forth. Seven is a significant number in the Bible. Seven in its primary meaning is completion. This, when combined with the context, means he continued to call the rain forth until there was a fullness of completion.

These scriptures contain a huge understanding for us as well. When we know the will of God, we should call that will forth and continue in that prophetic declaration, without changing our mind or speech, as it's being formed, until His will is manifest. This, says James, is the "prayer of Faith".

Can you see it now! In light of the scriptures and the model of Jesus, the "prayer of faith" is to declare God's will with authority knowing that you are acting on God's behalf or acting as He would have you to act (having given you dominion) in the earth.

IT IS TO REBUKE, TO SAY OR TO COMMAND!

You are not commanding God; you are using the knowledge of His will, His power resident in the name of His son and you are doing your part in bringing the Kingdom of God on the earth as it is in heaven.

Matthew 6:9 "Pray, then, in this way...10
'Thy kingdom come. Thy will be done, On
earth as it is in heaven.

Note the two categories where you are a deputy
sheriff and law enforcement agent

1. Acting as He would act, on His behalf, as if He were present.   As if you were Him.

   Take some time and fill in some examples.

2. Acting as He would have you to act as an heir of God in the earth.

   Write down some ways you can implement these strategies for victory right now:

WHAT IF FAITH DOESN'T WORK?

John 5:19 Jesus therefore answered and was saying to them, "Truly, truly, I say to you, the Son can do nothing of Himself, unless it is something He sees the Father doing; for whatever the Father does, these things the Son also does in like manner.

Someone came to me and said, "Pastor I know all about this teaching and I've tried it before and it didn't work."

How about you, have you tried this?

My first comment is that **you can't <u>try</u> this method of prayer**. I know what you mean when you say you tried it, but you must make up your mind about the Word of God regardless of circumstances...you either believe and act or you don't. But to be fair with this argument, how many of us have tried using this "prayer of faith and authority" before and not seen it work? Probably many Christians at one time or another.

To be honest, all of us had felt this way about spiritual things at one point or another. But let me ask you, how good were you with a shovel when you were young?

I have four little children and my boys especially love tools. The little one is out in the garage all the time trying to cut or hammer. But my kids have a terrible time with a shovel and they could probably dig better with a hammer. Should they continue to dig with a hammer as they grow up and get strong? How good are children with a skill saw?

They could probably shave a 2x4 down easier with a belt sander or a block plane right now?

You get my point. That is just because you are not proficient with a certain tool doesn't mean it's not the right tool for the job. It also doesn't mean you should not learn to use the proper tool. The right tool is often difficult to use, and it might require more skill and maturity, but it's well worth it in the end.

Likewise, there might be some reasons why "commanding" "saying" and "rebuking" did not work for you in the past. The "prayer of faith" should work and people should be raised up, but we have to practice.

> *Hebrews 5:14 But solid food is for the mature, who because of practice have their senses trained to discern good and evil.*

Let's look at four reasons given for failure and build up our scriptural knowledge in each of these important areas. If we discover why the prayer of authority might not bring the desired results we'll get the knowledge we need to move mountains.

THE ABIDING IN CHRIST FACTOR...

*John 15:7 "**If ye abide in me**, and my words abide in you, ye shall ask what ye will, and it shall be done unto you." "By this My Father is glorified, that you bear much fruit; so you will be My disciples."*

The first phrase I want us to focus in on is the phrase; "If ye abide in me"

<u>Abide</u> is defined in the Strong's exhaustive concordance as word #3306. Meaning to stay (in a given place, state, relation or expectancy):--abide, continue, dwell, endure, be present, remain, stand, tarry (for), X thine own.

He is telling the disciples that if they want to have unlimited answers to prayer they have to abide in Him.

By meaning, He is saying if you <u>continue in me</u>, <u>dwell in me</u>, <u>endure in me</u>, <u>live present in me</u>, <u>remain in me</u>, <u>stand in me</u>, <u>tarry in me</u>...

So in light of the meaning of Abide, let's look at the first requirement to success in the prayer of faith and authority. The first requirement is to abide in Christ. Here we find the first criteria to the prayer of faith.

What is He saying? How would they have received this saying? What else would they abide in?

For these listeners they were used to abiding in works and abiding in the law. They counted themselves righteous by their fulfilling of the law, which, we're told was impossible.

If your position of righteousness with God was impossible imagine how that would affect your confidence and authority. Authority with God and as His delegate is based on your position of righteousness. Therefore, if the position of righteousness wavers, so does your authority as a deputy.

He is telling them something they didn't understand until later, that they would have their life in Him and their relationship with the Father would be based on the sacrifice of His life in their place.

He is talking about right relationship. Paul explained it by saying that we have been given the righteousness of Jesus.

2 Corinthians 5: 21 He made Him who

knew no sin to be sin on our behalf, that
we might become the righteousness of
God in Him.

This is a totally different concept and mind set than abiding in self, abiding in knowledge, abiding in pride or abiding in false gods and outside of Christ.

Abiding in Christ is abiding under the covering of His righteousness, finding your identity in Him, being hidden in Him, covered by Him, resting in Him.

This state of faith is what gives the believer authority over all things. Jesus is the supreme one, triumphant over death, hell and the grave. He has been given all authority in heaven and on earth and under the earth. When you are hidden in Him, hidden in His righteousness you stand in His authority.

You will never move into the mountain moving, demon conquering, curse overcoming realm without abiding in Christ completely, and coming to know that you are covered by His righteousness.

The righteous continue in faith.

Galatians 3:10-14

The righteous walk as sons.
Romans 8:14-16

The righteous are led by the spirit.
Rom. 8:15

The righteous know they are covered by the Lord.
2 Corinthians 5:21
The righteous will reign in life.
Romans 5:17
The righteous will keep their hearts pure.
1 John 1:9

Are you abiding in Him and trusting in Him completely or are you following Him when it is easy and convenient?

1   2   3   4   5   6   7   8   9   10

What is keeping you from a full trust?
- Fear of rejection?

- Fear of failing?
- Fear He won't provide for you?

Write your own notes of what the Lord is now showing you:

THE RHEMA FACTOR

*"... and **my words** abide in you, ye shall ask what ye will, and it shall be done unto you."*

In this portion of the scripture we're examining the phrase, and my words abide in you.

"Words" is defined in the Strongs exhaustive concordance as #4487. In the greek it is the word **rhema**, hray'-mah; from G4483; an **utterance** (individ., collect. or spec.); by impl. a matter or topic (espec. of narration, command or dispute); with a neg. naught whatever: --+ evil, + nothing, saying, word.

The word in the Greek for is "rhema." You can see from the Strongs concordance that the word "rhema" means the **utterance** of God, the narrative of God, the saying of God.

Here in this passage Jesus was telling the disciples that the next key to move mountains with the prayer of faith and authority is that **His Word** must abide in you...not your words, not someone else's words, not the word of Aunt Mildred, not the preacher who never saw mountains move or clouds form.

Rhema means the word from God that is "alive" to you, revealed to you, as if God spoke it to you in the present tense...fresh manna, a living thing from God Himself.

The "rhema" must **abide in you** for you to command what you will and it to be done for you. Jesus spoke of this in John 5:19.

"Logos" is another Greek word for God's Word, but it differs in that it refers to the written Word of God.

The Logos outlines the general sphere of God's word and His will, but the Logos is not enough for you to develop or sustain mountain moving faith. First you must have "a word" from God. A Word from God must become life to you, made a "rhema".

For us to exercise faith and dominion in specific situations, we need a rhema word from God. It's not enough to know scriptures so as to quote them, or to know scriptures by memory. We have in our culture theologians who know the Word of God **mentally** but have a life void of great fruit. It's not enough to know **about** the Word of God. Growing up in Church I knew virtually every Bible story, yet I was lacking the faith to move mountains.

The Word must become faith within you personally. You must have had a Word quickened or made alive by the Holy Spirit for you to have mountain moving faith.

For instance. You might know that Jesus wants to build **the Church** and win **all souls**, but that does not mean you are "called" to plant a church. Being "called" means you have heard a direct "rhema" word from the Lord and understand what He wanted you to do.

You might read about Jesus healing the sick and casting out demons, but not receive the revelation of that same power being given to you. At some point in prayer or by a "touch" of the Holy Spirit upon your life you will come to know you are called to do exactly what He did. These specific revelations can't happen to you until the Holy Spirit causes His Word to come alive to you. This is when a word becomes "rhema" to you.

This "quickening" happens by the grace of God as you study, worship, seek Him, learn and hear the Word of God. Just lifting up Jesus Christ in worship can bring about a liberty that will lift a mental veil of doubt or ignorance. In just a flash God has spoken to me in the midst of Worship and made me to know something in the Spirit.

In II Corinthians 3:15-18 we are told that where the spirit of Jesus is welcomed, there comes a liberty to perceive and understand the scriptures.

> 2 Corinthians 3:15 But to this day
> whenever Moses is read, a veil lies over
> their heart;
> but whenever a man turns to the Lord, the
> veil is taken away. Now the Lord is the

*Spirit; and where the Spirit of the Lord is,
there is liberty.*

Sometimes the logos, or scriptures, are made relevant to you by the Holy Spirit-- as it pertains to something specific in your life.   In this process the <u>Logos is becoming Rhema</u>. A written word is becoming alive and an utterance of God to you for that moment or for a relevant time.

At other times, God speaks to you personally by the spirit with spiritual thoughts and spiritual words perceived within the heart.

When the Holy Spirit "quickens" a word to you, it will result in hope and faith.

*Romans 15:4 For whatever was written in
earlier times was written for our
instruction, that through perseverance
and the encouragement of the Scriptures
we might have hope.*

I Corinthians 2: 12 Now we have received,

*not the spirit of the world, but the Spirit
who is from God, that we might know the
things freely given to us by God, which
things we also speak, not in words taught
by human wisdom, but in those taught by
the Spirit, combining spiritual thoughts
with spiritual words.*

Lots of people have missed God and the power of commanding something to come to pass because they did not FIRST hear the Word of the Lord for their situation. Faith you create on your own is different than the faith that Gods gives you through His Word. True authoritative faith comes by hearing the Rhema of God.

The reason Jesus never failed in His faith was that He always heard the Father.   Therefore, the Father always heard Him. The Word was abiding in Him.

*John 5:19 Jesus therefore answered and
was saying to them, "Truly, truly, I say to
you, the Son can do nothing of Himself,
unless it is something He sees the Father
doing; for whatever the Father does, these
things the Son also does in like manner.*

John 11: 41 Then they took away the stone
from the place where the dead was laid.
And Jesus lifted up his eyes, and said,
Father, I thank thee that thou hast heard
me. 42 And I knew that thou hearest me
always:
John 12:50 "And I know that His
commandment is eternal life; therefore
the things I speak, I speak just as the
Father has told Me."

Cherishing the Word, giving the word an abiding place is how Ezekiel responded to the Holy Spirit.

Ezekiel 37:1 The hand of the LORD was
upon me, and He brought me out by the
Spirit of the LORD and set me down in the
middle of the valley; and it was full of
bones. And He caused me to pass among
them round about, and behold, there were
very many on the surface of the valley;
and lo, they were very dry. And He said to
me, "Son of man, can these bones live?"
And I answered, "O Lord GOD, Thou
knowest." 4 Again He said to me,
"Prophesy over these bones, and say to

them, 'O dry bones, hear the word of the LORD.'

When you are in a storm, a wilderness or up against a mountain, you need a Word from the Lord. He is the one who can give you the "word" to turn everything around, because His Word is the basis for faith.

Faith is the basis for change and creative power.

Can you think of a time when this would have helped you?

You'll notice that Ezekiel looked to God. God is the one who gives life to the dead and calls things in to being that don't exist.

Romans 4: 17 As it is written: "I have made you a father of many nations." He is our father in the sight of God, in whom he believed--the God who gives life to the dead and calls things that are not as though they were. NIV

Now in your life, like with Ezekiel and Elijah, He wants to empower you with the power of His word to change some things.

- Are you complaining about your mountain, or speaking to it?
- What are your mountains?

When a true Rhema happens by revelation from God, faith will be the immediate result.

Faith is the absence of fear.

Faith is a confidence in a positive outcome, should you believe and act upon your belief.

Fear is believing that you'll have to submit to the circumstances, that things are hopeless.

Faith is a testimony from God that circumstances can be changed.

> Romans 10:17 So then faith cometh by hearing, and hearing by the **word** (Rhema) of God.

His Word is described as being "born of Him." John says if something from God is the basis of our faith, then our faith will overcome any obstacle.

> *I John 5:4 For whatsoever is born of God overcometh the world: and this is the victory that overcometh the world, even our faith.*

Strongs defines **Born** as word #1080. gennao, ghen-nah'-o; from a variation of G1085; to procreate (prop. of the father, but by extens. of the mother); figuratively to regenerate:--bear, beget, be born, bring forth, conceive, be delivered of, gender, make, spring.

Some great ideas that come to our minds aren't born of God. Some mountain moving ideas that come to our minds aren't born of God. In such a case we might have a great ambition for a good thing, but the power of God won't back us up.

We always need to judge each good mountain moving idea against the scripture and against the rhema Words that we have received. For instance, many Christians have misused Philippians 4:13.

*Philippians 4:13 I can do **all** things
through Him who strengthens me.*

For years Christians have used this verse out of context to justify any and everything they wanted to do. This verse doesn't imply you can do **anything**, because we have to interpret the statement in the larger context of the passage.

*Philippians 4:12 I know how to get along
with humble means, and I also know how
to live in prosperity; in any and every
circumstance I have learned the secret of
being filled and going hungry, both of
having abundance and suffering need. 13
I can do all things through Him who
strengthens me.*

In the context of the verse Paul implies you can do anything God calls you do! Paul was able to all God called him to. Paul was able to succeed while abounding and he was able to succeed while abased. God's Word must be preeminent in all things. There are ditches on both sides of the road. One ditch is to be attempting to move mountains, but you've not received a rhema word from the Lord.

The other ditch is to never do anything unless you have a personal visitation from God for each individual situation. This too is an error and an imbalance.

Once you understand the nature of God's will by a rhema word, you don't need a new rhema when you come up to the same mountain again. Jesus showed us this truth when He manifested Fathers will to heal and raise the dead. Once He had that rhema He could dispense that power as needed.

> John 5: 19 Jesus therefore answered and was saying to them, "Truly, truly, I say to you, the Son can do nothing of Himself, unless it is something He sees the Father doing; for whatever the Father does, these things the Son also does in like manner. 20 "For the Father loves the Son, and shows Him all things that He Himself is doing; and greater works than these will He show Him, that you may marvel. 21 "For just as the Father raises the dead and gives them life, <u>even so the Son also gives life to whom He wishes.</u>

Patience is our next key to mountain moving faith and authority.

159

If you really hear from God you'll be able to hold on to that revelation all the way through the period of resistance and conflict.

This, true hearing from God, has sustained me when everything in the natural was shouting "give up". It's knowing that I heard from God that stabilized me and gave me a foundation to withstand the storm.

THE PATIENCE FACTOR

*"...and my words **abide** in you, ye shall ask what ye will, and it shall be done unto you."*

In this section of study we'll look at the next part of this mountain moving phrase. Here Jesus said His words must ABIDE in us. If the enemy can resist you for a period of time, he's often able to get you to pull back your assault or position with your own confession. The Hebrew writer says:

"Hold fast your confession of faith."

Hebrews 3:6

In other words, don't let go of what you demanded, don't let go of what you desired and required.

God's Word must "abide" in you permanently if you are going to bear fruit. Satan will try to get you off of the Word that God has given you. He wants that word out of your heart. Jesus said persecution even arises because of the Word.

> *Matthew 13: 20 "And the one on whom seed was sown on the rocky places, this is the man who hears the word, and immediately receives it with joy; 21 yet he has no firm root in himself, but is only temporary, and when affliction or persecution arises because of the word, immediately he falls away.*

When God gives you a Word get ready for warfare, but more importantly, get ready to win ground if you stand your ground.

Remember our understanding of **Abide:** defined in Strongs #3306. meno, men'-o; **a prim. verb**; to stay (in a given place, state, relation or expectancy):--abide, continue, dwell, endure, be present, remain, stand, tarry (for), X thine own.

Satan will work to deceive you and wear you out with delay and during a delay of seeing the word fulfilled. Scripture after scripture implies that you must keep applying a steadfast pressure to your mountain. That steadfast, unwavering pressure is patience.

*Hebrews. 6:12 do not become sluggish, but imitate those who through faith and **patience** inherit the promises.*

Consider the principle of the seed. One reason for patience is because the Word of God is like a seed. Seeds don't bear fruit over night. When you first walk by your garden you don't see any indication that you planted seed there. You may be tempted to tear the whole thing up and put in a sport court...but just wait. Keep tending it, keep watering it and soon you'll see the little sprout of what you've been saying and prophesying.

Mark 4:26 And He was saying, "The

kingdom of God is like a man who casts seed upon the soil; and goes to bed at night and gets up by day, and the seed sprouts up and grows-- how, he himself does not know. For the earth bringeth forth fruit of herself; first the blade, then the ear, after that the full corn in the ear.

A common problem with all of God's servants is impatience. Impatience got Abraham and Sarah in trouble and it has tripped up the best humans since then. You'll remember that he went in to lay with Hagar because Sarah was not bringing forth the promised son. Most of us have a much shorter timeline then God. I'm sure Joseph was a little tempted to doubt God during the 13 years of delay he experienced. Early on in our ministry I was blessed to hear from God.

This happened in my car on the way home from a church meeting. It was as if the Holy Spirit came into my car that night and talked to me. He told me it would be 10 years for the vision He'd given me to come to fulfillment. This intimate time with God for just a few moments sustained me through years of hard times. It has made me think of the words of James a little different.

James writes that if you need wisdom about the trial you are going through, then ask God and He'll give you wisdom.

> James 1:2 Consider it all joy, my brethren,
> when you encounter various trials,
> knowing that the testing of your faith
> produces endurance. And let endurance
> have its perfect result, that you may be
> perfect and complete, lacking in nothing.
> But if any of you lacks wisdom, let him ask
> of God, who gives to all men generously
> and without reproach, and it will be given
> to him.

Many times, you might not understand why you are going through a trial. You don't have the wisdom of God on it, you don't know how long it might go on or how to overcome it. James says that in those dark times you can seek God for insights to sustain us.

How about you? Have you been tempted to retreat? Have you been tempted to scale down your dream because it just doesn't look like it's going to come to pass?

Ask God first, really seek Him with all your heart and He will give wisdom to all who ask in faith.

I am convinced that the reason many spiritual leaders don't do a significant work for God is that they do not stay at it long enough and hard enough in one location to win. Sometimes it's the fault of the denomination or organization. Likewise, most Christians don't stay with their dream.

We have to remember, most principalities that we face have been entrenched for a good long time, just as the seven unclean nations had been in the promise land for 430 years. They occupy the powers of the lower atmosphere when pastors and spiritual leaders come to a city to lead a people for God.

Demonic strongmen have had their way for a good long time and they are used to that scenario. They are usually entrenched in government, in the church and in families. They are not going to give up easy, because they have learned over time how easy it is to move out even the best spiritual leaders.

Most pastors come to a city and stay just long enough to confront or contact the principality and the warfare of the principality. Most the time no real impact is made on tearing down the principality, because before a real powerful impact can be made they resign or wear out.

Keys to the abiding patience that bears fruit.

- You will not retreat on what you have said.
- You will not be discouraged. (Joshua 1: 6-8)
- You will not focus on circumstances that dismay or contradict.
- You will not listen to evil reports. (Psalm 1:1-3)
- You will not quit moving ahead and working like it's coming to pass.
- You will have a plan and work your plan based on the Word regardless of feeling
- You will not change your mind.
- You will not be threatened, adversity just causes more resolve. (James 1:1-4)
- You will keep you focus on the joy set before you when the fruit comes. (Hebrews 12:1,2)
- You will not take on timidity, fear of cautiousness. (2 Timothy 1:7)
- You will keep rejoicing in your God and His ability to prevail (Romans 4:20,21)

If Satan discovers how to buy you off or wear you out, watch out. In the future he'll use the same tactic over and over again. No matter what comes you have to decide you are not going to release the rhema Word that God gave you.

> *Mountain movers will be those who learn from adversity, rather than become overwhelmed by it. Adversity comes to destroy those who could have won the war.*

The bible says though a righteous man falls seven times he gets back up. This verse is talking about a righteous man. Therefore, this passage doesn't mean the falling to sin so much as it means the falling to adversity. A righteous man might have difficulty and delay, but he presses on according to the Word.

> *Proverbs 24:16 For a righteous man falls seven times, and rises again, But the wicked stumble in time of calamity.*

We must learn to develop a sense of winning through adversity, because that is precisely how winning comes. Many people have conditioned themselves to give up in the face of adversity because they give up over the little things. Jesus said, if you are faithful in the small things, then you'll be faithful in the great.

> Luke 8: 15 *"And the seed in the good soil,*
> *these are the ones who have heard the*
> *word in an honest and good heart, and*
> *hold it fast, and bear fruit with*
> *perseverance.*

THE EXPERIENCE FACTOR

> *"...and my words abide in you, ye shall ask*
> *what ye will, and it shall be done unto*
> *you."*

There is nothing like the joy and confidence in your God like that which comes as a result God blessing you and backing up your faith in Him. This is faith becoming sight. As my faith has become sight, I've gotten even more encouraged for the next battle and more humbled by the awesome power of my God.

- I've seen God provide for us financially

- I've seen God deliver us from property claims against us
- I've seen God shut the mouth of opposition
- I've seen God give us favor and honor in our City
- I've seen demons cast out and sent fleeing

Now my confidence is even stronger with regard to other things that God has told us to do and to pray. The same thing will happen to you.

David's confidence to take on a giant was built partially upon the victories God had given him with a lion and a bear. Victories are progressive and become larger as you become a faith-filled warrior. That is why you shouldn't despise the day of small beginnings (With God nothing that starts small will stay small).

> *1 Samuel 17:33 Then Saul said to David, "You are not able to go against this Philistine to fight with him; for you are but a youth while he has been a warrior from his youth." But David said to Saul, "Your servant was tending his father's sheep. When **a lion or a bear** came and took a lamb from the flock, I went out after him and attacked him, and rescued it from his mouth; and when he rose up*

against me, I seized him by his beard and struck him and killed him. "Your servant has killed both the lion and the bear; and this uncircumcised Philistine will be like one of them, since he has taunted the armies of the living God." And David said, "The LORD who delivered me from the paw of the lion and from the paw of the bear, He will deliver me from the hand of this Philistine." And Saul said to David, "Go, and may the LORD be with you."

- God prepares David for a Giant with a lion and a bear.

- God prepares Joseph for national leadership with a pit, with Potiphar and with prison.

- God prepares Moses for delivering a nation with shepherding sheep in Midian.

- God prepares Gideon for the Midianites with treading out some grain in secret.

For this reason, I say use your authority all the time. Build your faith by using it even in small situations and problems.

- Don't wait for cancer to attack your body, use the prayer of faith to rebuke cold germs and flu bugs.

- Cast fear off of your children.
- Don't wait for the worst calamities to strike, set the course of your life with your words.
- Declare the will of God over your family members, your community and city.

A testimony is a praise report that has come out of a test. When you have gone through a fiery test and you hold fast until victory then you have a testimony. No one can steal the testimony that will result.

In Revelation John records that the saints will overcome the enemy "by the word of their testimony." (Revelation 11:12). When you share your testimony then Satan knows that you know what God did when He delivered you. If you don't give your testimony, then Satan isn't nearly as terrified of your reputation. Along these lines God instructed the Children of Israel to erect memorials of their victories, so that they would remember and so they would give the testimony to their children and their children's children.

> *Joshua 4: 5 ...and Joshua said to them,*
> *"Cross again to the ark of the LORD your*
> *God into the middle of the Jordan, and*

each of you take up a stone on his
shoulder, according to the number of the
tribes of the sons of Israel. "Let this be a
sign among you, so that when your
children ask later, saying, 'What do these
stones mean to you?' then you shall say to
them, 'Because the waters of the Jordan
were cut off before the ark of the covenant
of the LORD; when it crossed the Jordan,
the waters of the Jordan were cut off.' So,
these stones shall become a memorial to
the sons of Israel forever."

Likewise, you should not forget what God has done for you! Write every victory down with the date in your bible journal book and review those victories for encouragement!

So, you see acting on the Word not only gives you confidence in God, but it also makes you known to your enemy. The more victories through the power of His Word, the more your reputation grows in the spirit realm. I personally want to be known in the courts of Satan.

As your reputation grows, successive things begin to crumble under your feet with greater ease. Paul had become known to demons just as Jesus had become known. Not that someone could have cast out a demon in the name of Paul. But Paul, by using the name of Jesus to defeat demons and demonic strongholds had a reputation with demons.

> *Acts 19:14 Also there were seven sons of Sceva, a Jewish chief priest, who did so. And the evil spirit answered and said,* ***"Jesus I know****, and* ***Paul I know****, but* ***who are you?****" Then the man in whom the evil spirit was leaped on them, overpowered them, and prevailed against them, so that they fled out of that house naked and wounded.*

FOUR FACTORS TO ENSURE GREATER VICTORIES

You'll need to keep all four of these factors in mind as you tackle the mountains, storms and enemies of your life.

These factors will help you stay your course and overcome time after time.

1. **Abiding** in Him
2. Seeking His pure Rhema **Word** for your life
3. **Holding** on to His Word patiently and steadfastly.
4. Building **victory** upon **victory**.

PUT YOUR AUTHORITY TO WORK TODAY

Where can you use this powerful tool of authority?

James 2:26 ...faith without action is dead!

USE YOUR AUTHORITY OVER NATURAL CIRCUMSTANCES

When Adam and Eve were created, they were given authority over all of the earth. They had dominion over all things. Dominion over animals, dominion over weather, dominion over crops, dominion over sickness and demons...dominion over all things. This is why Jesus, the last Adam, operated in this same authority.

> *Genesis 1: 28 And God blessed them, and God said unto them, Be fruitful, and multiply, and replenish the earth, and subdue it: and have dominion over the fish of the sea, and over the fowl of the air, and over every living thing that moveth upon the earth. (KJV)*

When Jesus spoke to storms and cursed trees he wasn't doing anything that Adam couldn't have done in the beginning. Jesus was the "last Adam." He didn't do these works just to show off. He did these works to show us the power and authority we have when we live in the earth submitted to God almighty.

I've spoken to storms and commanded them to move and God has backed me up and moved the storm.

On a vacation for the Lord, I spoke against all odds and caught a Swordfish because God caused it to obey me.

My wife and I were on a vacation visit to Cabo San Lucas in the Baja of Mexico. One morning we decided to go down to the marina and see if we could find a fishing boat that would be affordable. We were thinking about going out and doing some deep sea fishing. We bargained with a couple of the locals for a while and finally contracted with the owners of a boat to take us our for five hours, but that meant that we could only go eight miles out before we would have to return. We were really excited about getting a 42' boat all to ourselves.

As we climbed on board I got more and more excited about catching a Marlin (Sword fish), but all the way out the skipper told us that the Marlin's were being caught at 25 miles out. He was on his radio and confirming with other boat owners where the Marlin's were that day. We were catching several fish as we were headed out to 8 miles, but no Marlin. We were catching tuna and Mai-Mai, but I still wanted a Marlin. As went got underway I got serious about this and started using my faith. I began to see a Marlin on my pole and I began to call a Marlin to my hook. By faith I also was telling the skipper I would catch one.

Time went by and time went by and no Marlin. The crew was getting disappointed as we went along. They too wanted me to catch one, but they saw it wasn't going to happen. All along I just kept saying yes I will catch a marlin. Throughout the trip I held on to the image and faith that I would catch a Marlin. Then in the last few seconds before the skipper had to turn the boat around and head back to harbor God sent me a 9' Marlin. Suddenly it was on my line and the wild ride was on. Reeling it in and working it to the boat was 25 minutes of sheer excitement. The reel was called a "beast tamer" and what a beast we had. Soon it was up and, in the boat,...125lbs of Marlin. We were shouting and screaming because God brought us a Marlin.

Everybody was stunned. It was unbelievable, yet true. God had given an inner word, honored my "prayer of faith and authority" and met me with a miracle.

I exhort you to put the Lord to the test in this area and watch your faith grow.

Paul tells us that the whole of creation is waiting to work with the Sons of God and to be delivered from futility. Creation has been made to work with you, not against you, but you have to start acting like a Son of God in the earth.

The Lord will meet you when you live this way. When the Lord meets you with signs and wonders stay humble.

Don't take on pride, don't put others down. Don't get up on soap box. Use the situation to glorify Jesus and gently make the truth known.

USE YOUR AUTHORITY TO HEAL THE SICK

When you go to pray for the sick, go in the authority of Jesus. Quietly ask the Holy Spirit for insights that go beyond your natural understanding.

- There might be demons of infirmity holding the person.
- There might be unforgiveness toward another person.
- Are there demons who need to be cast out?
- There might be visible signs of sickness, but an underlying root cause.

You might consider quietly praying and listening for instructions from the Holy Spirit.

Once you feel you have prepared yourself and submitted to the chief physician then begin to pray.

Take authority over the sickness and cast it off and out of the person. Take authority over demons and cast them off and out of the person. Command that the hindrances and afflictions against the flesh cease.

If you need, as Jesus did, gently ask the people who might have doubt or unbelief to leave the room. I have seen many people touched and healed as I have prayed the prayer of faith over them.

After you have prayed fervently for a while and destroyed the sickness and it's root you should release restoration over the person. Lift up your voice and command the restoration of Jesus to take over their entire body. You have the authority to call the things are aren't into being and to give life to dead things with your mouth.

Romans 4: 17 "...even God, who gives life to the dead and calls into being that which does not exist."

USE YOUR AUTHORITY TO DISPLACE PRINCIPALITIES, POWERS AND WORLD RULERS.

According the Smith Bible dictionary, the gates and gateways of ancient cities held an important role for each City. (Pg. 207) They were sometimes taken as representing the very City itself and all that was encompassed in a City/ Region. This could have been where "principalities" first dominated in culture. The word "principalities" seen in Ephesians 6 and means "first one" or the one in "first place".

Ephesians 6:12 For we wrestle not against flesh and blood, but against <u>principalities</u>, against powers, against the rulers of the darkness of this world, against spiritual wickedness in high places. KJV

The gate was the central point of rule in the ancient day and in the ancient day Satan was the "prince and the power of the air" the "ruler of darkness" who held the "world systems" in his control.

It was at the gate of a city and each geographic capitol that Satan would have ruled or held sway over the influencers. We might say that whoever controlled the gates controlled the whole city/ region and the people of the city/ region.

Daniel 10:13 "But the <u>prince of the kingdom of Persia was withstanding me</u> for twenty-one days; then behold, Michael, one of the chief princes, came to help me, for I had been left there with the kings of Persia.

Throughout history, in gentile cities, it was common for the leaders at the gate to be covetous, biased, prejudiced, perverse and thus demonized. Therefore, their influence skewed all that happened at the gates.

Here is a brief overview of the activities happening at the gates of the ancient City:

- Administration of justice and governmental rule
- Public market, distribution and bartering
- Discussion, debate and exchange of ideas
- Heathen sacrifice and worship
- Slave trade, hiring
- Prostitution, marriage and divorce
- Protection and defense
- Entertainment and amusement

Later in history we see this as being synonymous with the "town square" or "public square".

In this day, though we don't have one formal gate where all leadership is represented, but we do have gate keepers in every City, County, State and Nation.

Gatekeepers are human leaders, corporations and entities who are led by the Holy Spirit or led the by influence from the "gates of Hell". Some of these gate keepers may be found in the County-City buildings and others in state capitols, as many gate keepers of society are dispersed throughout a region.

Why do we say gatekeepers are dispersed throughout a region? Because governmental rule is only one sphere of influence in any society.

Again, look at the list of the activities that transpired at the ancient gate. For each item there are "gatekeepers" or chief influencers. Therefore, we can't affect change in government only and expect all of society or culture to change.

Admittedly and thankfully in the United States we've come a long way from the day of demon dominion that was common with other nations throughout history. Since the inception of our nation and until 1960 we were blessed with a strong Christian influence at the gates.

Since 1960 we can now see a clearly devised plan of Satan has been released to take back the gates and thus the seats of influence. This came as Christians just in time from Satan's perspective, as Christians were giving so much heed to rapture theology they were retreating from every gate – sphere and sector of culture.

Clearly, we've seen a resurgence of greed, perversity, sodomy, whoredoms, godlessness, idolatry, false religion, atheism, evolution, pluralism, etc. All of this flowing out of our gatekeepers and their platforms of influence.

Why? Because our gatekeepers are operating from the power, wisdom and influence that comes from the "gates of Hell".

I want to suggest that we, the body of Christ, are called to capture the leadership of all that was represented at the ancient gates. The gates of God's power and wisdom are meant to prevail against the gates of Hell.

Look at Paul's comments on this very topic.

I Corinthians 1:20 Where is the wise man? Where is the scribe? Where is the debater of this age? Has not God made foolish the wisdom of the world?
I Corinthians 1:25 Because the foolishness of God is wiser than men, and the weakness of God is stronger than men. 26 For consider your calling, brethren, that there were not many wise according to the flesh, not many mighty, not many noble;

*27 but God has chosen the foolish things
of the world to shame the wise, and God
has chosen the weak things of the world to
shame the things which are strong, 28
and the base things of the world and the
despised, God has chosen, the things that
are not, that He might nullify the things
that are, 29 that no man should boast
before God.*

Jesus made a radical statement about our God given rule and dominion.

*Matthew 16:18 "And I also say to you that
you are Peter, and upon this rock I will
build My church; and the gates of Hades
shall not overpower it.*

Herein Jesus essentially was declaring that the ungodly rule and authority of Satan's kingdom would no longer prevail against the rule of the righteous in the earth. In this scripture He is setting the Church in an adversarial relationship with the gates (rule, authority, leadership) of Satan, stating that the Church shall **prevail**.

"Prevail" is a military term. "Prevail" suggests aggression, conflict and war.

Here He could have said...

"the rule of Hell shall not overpower the Church (God's ambassadors of His Kingdom)."

"the counsel of Hell shall not overpower Church."

"the leadership and influence of Hell shall not overpower the Church."

"the wisdom and philosophy of Hell shall not overpower the Church."

Additional scriptures speak about the time in which we are living and declare that:

The House of the Lord will be established as the chief house and the chief mountain...

Micah 4:1 And it will come about in the last days That the mountain of the house of the LORD Will be established as the chief of the mountains. It will be raised above the hills, And the peoples will stream to it. 2 And many nations will come and say, "Come and let us go up to the mountain of the LORD And to the house of the God of Jacob, That He may teach us about His ways And that we may walk in His paths." For from Zion will go

forth the law, Even the word of the LORD
from Jerusalem.

The increase of His government over all things will have no end until all be subdued under Jesus...

> *Isaiah 9: 6 For a child will be born to us, a son will be given to us; And the government will rest on His shoulders; And His name will be called Wonderful Counselor, Mighty God, Eternal Father, Prince of Peace. 7 There will be no end to the increase of His government or of peace, On the throne of David and over his kingdom, To establish it and to uphold it with justice and righteousness From then on and forevermore. The zeal of the LORD of hosts will accomplish this.*

Jesus is seated at the right hand of the Father until all enemies are subdued...

> *Hebrews 1:13 But to which of the angels has He ever said, "SIT AT MY RIGHT HAND, UNTIL I MAKE THINE ENEMIES A FOOTSTOOL FOR THY FEET"?*

Jesus is now ruling from heavenly Jerusalem...

Hebrews 12:22 But you have come to Mount Zion and to the city of the living God, the heavenly Jerusalem, and to myriads of angels, 23 to the general assembly and church of the first-born who are enrolled in heaven, and to God, the Judge of all, and to the spirits of righteous men made perfect, 24 and to Jesus, the mediator of a new covenant, and to the sprinkled blood, which speaks better than the blood of Abel.

Through the Church the authority of Jesus is to be revealed to principalities and powers...

Ephesians 3: 8 Although I am less than the least of all God's people, this grace was given me: to preach to the Gentiles the unsearchable riches of Christ, 9 and to make plain to everyone the administration of this mystery, which for ages past was kept hidden in God, who created all things. 10 His intent was that now, <u>through the church</u>, the manifold wisdom of God should be made known to the rulers and authorities in the heavenly realms, 11 according to his eternal purpose which he accomplished in Christ Jesus our **Lord. NIV**

We rule and reign in life through Christ Jesus...

> *Romans 5:17 For if by the transgression of the one, death reigned through the one, much more those who receive the abundance of grace and of the gift of righteousness will reign in life through the One, Jesus Christ.*

The righteous will inherit the land, but the wicked will be cast out...

> *Psalm 37: 9 For evildoers will be cut off, But those who wait for the LORD, they will inherit the land. 10 Yet a little while and the wicked man will be no more; And you will look carefully for his place, and he will not be there. 11 But the humble will inherit the land, And will delight themselves in abundant prosperity.*

It is clear from scripture that the Body of Christ is to grow into the prevailing body of influence in the World. But how?

We should know from scripture and military prowess that the best defense is a strong offense. We cannot prevail with regard to the "gates" of Satanic wisdom, rule and leadership without war, but the war can't be fought purely against a nebulous enemy for world dominion.

Addressing Satan alone is certainly too broad, confusing and will not bring victory. We need micro and macro strategies of dominion.

The war of displacement is won person by person and territory by territory. We are called to be the Josephs and Daniel's of our day. We will need to employ several strategies to "prevail" over these gate keepers.

A "strongman" at the "gate" guards a "stronghold" of wrong thinking and thus models of wrong behavior.

For total victory we (the Church) must return to a holistic battle approach.

First, we must identify the spheres of cultural influence (from the gates).

Second, we must differentiate between right and wrong (defining righteousness).

Third we must, in prophetic authority, confront the spiritual strongmen who influence our gates...tearing them down and casting them out. Prevailing, prophetic prayer will dislodge the demon led "gatekeepers" making place for the righteous of God to step into places of leadership and influence.

Fourth we, the Church, must declare the dominion of Jesus over our gates ...calling the gates restored and rebuilt into what God has ordained for them.

Fifth, we the Church, must seize our place in culture, modeling and teaching righteous behavior and the excellence of the King in each sphere of life.

The gates of today can be summarized through the following spheres of influence.

1. Religion, church
2. Sexuality, Marriage and Family
3. Education, Higher learning and philosophy
4. Tribes, Government and Law
5. Media and Communication
6. Music and the arts
7. Business, economics and Finance.
8. Science, Medicine and Health
9. Recreation, amusement, entertainment

As we partner with Jesus for completely overpowering the "gates of Hell" we will see the influence of the King come into each of these spheres.

You can use this method of prayer with all demons regardless of the rank or position. You have all the authority of Christ Jesus. Evil has been progressing in the earth because haven't taken our place as the anointed to bind up the enemy and cast him out.

However, be cautioned, with world rulers and principalities there is great benefit with the prayer of more than one person. And it might take more than just a swift rebuke to affect a mountain moving result. One can send a thousand to flight, two ten thousand! (Lev. 26:8 Deut. 32:30) The prayers of agreement can bring great results against demonic forces.

Daniel's answer was withheld because of spiritual resistance against him. The war was won by spirits wrestling, partially because Daniel didn't give up! We have a great power and a great responsibility.

Daniel 10: 12 Then he said to me, "Do not be afraid, Daniel, for from the first day that you set your heart on understanding *this and on humbling yourself before your God, your words were heard, and I have come in response to your words. 13 "But the <u>prince of the kingdom of Persia was withstanding me</u> for twenty-one days; then behold, Michael, one of the chief princes, came to help me, for I had been left there with the kings of Persia.*

Since in Christ you have all authority, you can rebuke small demons of control and bondage and with the same authority you can rebuke princes over nations.

Wisdom would dictate that you take a demand – command - rebuke to the highest level or rank in the demonic army. If you are shooting missiles at the infantry and not the commanders you may never see things change in the natural realm.

Paul said our struggle is not with flesh and blood, but with several levels of demonic influence in the earth realm. It only makes military sense that you would find out the highest level of influence for any problem you are facing and take the battle to that level. This is a good military strategy.

Ephesians 6: 12 For our struggle is not

*against flesh and blood, but against the
rulers, against the powers, against the
world forces of this darkness, against the
spiritual forces of wickedness in the
heavenly places.*

Here in Ephesians Paul suggests that our enemy has levels of influence, or degrees of rule, much like our military.

The Bible says that we can learn how things are structured in the spiritual (invisible) by looking at the natural. Since that is the case we always want to ask this question when we are praying.

- What are the demons resisting the will of God?
- What is the highest level of authority I need to deal with so as to bring a death blow to Satan's plan and work?
- What are the subordinate levels of authority also, so I can deal a death blow to them as well?

These are the questions you ask the Holy Spirit, not demons. Don't get into talking to demons regardless of what opportunity might come about.

The Holy Spirit is the Spirit of truth and he will guide you into all truth. Our fellowship is to be with Him. If you need illumination on something hidden, then there are revelation gifts of the Spirit to guide you into truth.

See I Corinthians 12 to study the "Spiritual gifts."

As the Holy Spirit gives you guidance victory can be as easy as just saying what He says to say, therefore getting into agreement with Him.

#1 DISPLACING PRINCIPALITIES:

There are princes over nations as is described in Daniel. These are the "commanders" in charge of the evil in a nation and at the top level.

Strong's exhaustive concordance defines Princes: #746. Greek word; arche, ar-khay'; from G756; (prop. abstr.) a commencement, or (concr.) chief (in various applications of order, time, place or rank):--beginning, corner, (at the, the) <u>first (estate), magistrate, power, principality, principle, rule.</u>

One example of a principality would be the "prince" that we see in the book of Daniel. This might be a demon who would be given the assignment to influence a nation. Such a spirit would also have influence over people groups within a nation. So you might consider a "prince" as the governing power over <u>geographical area</u>, <u>ethnic group or both</u>. Can you note the leadership of different "spirits" in the nations?

- Early Europeans were known for idol worship and witchcraft.

- Modern Europeans are known for stoicism, distrust of God, unbelief and a veneration of knowledge.

- Native Americans have been known for alcoholism, idolatry and addictions.

- African nations known for tribal hatred, witchcraft, sexual sin, violence, hatred and fighting.

- Tibet known for spiritual fear, poverty, idolatry and subjection to demons "gods".

- Caribbean nations are known for Voodoo, witchcraft, poverty.

- India known for poverty, reincarnation and the worship of animals.

- China known for atheism, oppression, poverty and communism.

America is a nation with a specific philosophy. Some of our guiding philosophies are godly, some aren't.

America started as a God fearing, Godly nation. Blessings were released upon America and she is known for many of these blessings throughout the world.

- America is known as the land of opportunity
- America is known as the land of wealth
- America is known as the land of personal prosperity

We have backslid from the prayers and intentions of the founding fathers. Therefore, America has attributes like the church of Laodacia, one of the seven churches spoken of in (Rev 3:14)

- America is neither hot or cold.
- America is lukewarm.
- America has all the symptoms of 2 Timothy 3.
- America is rich and in need of nothing, having lost her first love.

And we, though being pious, we have denied the power of God. We don't really need Him because we are doing good on our own. The power of God scares America.

Since this is the case, we as believers have to watch for this "influence" in our lives and take it captive. We can't be seduced by the "spirit" of the world.

- Spiritual apathy can't be tolerated
- We are so blessed we don't need to pray for life to go well for us. Renounce this pride, independence and greed.
- American Christians don't pray unless they have a crisis. It takes a crisis to bring us to seek God. This is selfishness.
- We don't seek God for the needs of others. This is rebellion and selfishness.

Nationally there are several strongmen who wield great influence in America:

- Pride and independence
- Rebellion and self will
- Greed and covetousness
- Anti-Christ and idolatry (another Christ)
- Babylon, spiritual whoredom where other idols are welcomed
- Bigotry, racism, division

- Sexual immorality, seduction, whoredoms, Baal, adultery

Are you letting the agenda of the enemy influence you? If so, take authority over it and do combat in the spirit realm.

Using the pattern of Jeremiah, you can destroy and overthrow the princes of darkness with prophetic declaration. If one can send a thousand to flight, two can send ten thousand.

Outline the principalities that have control over the nation:

Outline the principalities that have control over your State:

Outline the principalities that have control over the ethic people in your region:

#2. DISPLACING POWERS:

There are "powers" who are spirits who have the authority to promote evil because of the sins of people. Sin (obedience to Satan's agenda) gives Satan place in the earth even though He is defeated.

Strong's defines Powers: 1849. exousia, ex-oo-see'-ah; from G1832 (in the sense of ability); privilege, i.e. (subj.) force, capacity, competency, freedom, or (obj.) mastery (concr. magistrate, superhuman, potentate, token of control), delegated influence: --authority, jurisdiction, liberty, power, right, strength.

- Powers or authorities are present wherever sin exists, their purpose is to preside over it with inspiration and power. You can feel the presence of powers at certain times where the pervading atmosphere is unclean; IE., rock concerts, secular dances, during certain movies or TV shows.

- Powers might be understood as a contrast or opposite to the anointing or "virtue" of God's presence.

- They promote the things that the "flesh" or "sinful nature" craves.

- These "powers" are the spirits that come to indwell people when they give themselves over to a bondage or sin or fall into error.

- These are spirits on assignment as the infantry in an army, to oppress mankind and indwell the unsaved.

- They have their authority on the basis of permission or consent.

- They are often passed from one generation to another through the "law of sin and death".

- Their authority or power is related to the sin a person steps into.

- They have purposes that coincide with the "works of the flesh" and the rejection, poverty, inferiority, fear, sickness and death brought through the fall and made clear in the curse. I.E., fear, pity, rejection, immorality, hatred, murder, deceit, anger, adultery, drunkenness, bitterness, rebellion, witchcraft, etc.

All of us have to contend against "powers" and all of us in-Christ can win. Prayer and intercession over a specific person can bring complete freedom.

Many Christian opened themselves up to demon powers before they came to Christ. Pure repentance and a sustained prayer of rebuke can drive the spirits out of a person and they can be set free.

This type or method of prayer is similar to the prophetic prayer of Jeremiah, just as we used it in confronting principalities.

Jesus also modeled this kind of prayer. Many of us have been applying this prophetic understanding to our nation and cities over the last decade. We've been rebuking demon spirits and casting them out of our territories. Now we understand we can cast demon powers off of people too.

Unsaved people are demon controlled and demon bound. It is not just the sins of the flesh that hold the unsaved. The Bible says that they are blinded by the god of this world.

> *II Corinthians 4: 4:1 Therefore, since we have this ministry, as we received mercy, we do not lose heart, 2 but we have renounced the things hidden because of shame, not walking in craftiness or adulterating the word of God, but by the manifestation of truth commending ourselves to every man's conscience in the*

*sight of God. 3 And even if our gospel is
veiled, it is veiled to those who are
perishing, 4 in whose case the god of this
world has blinded the minds of the
unbelieving, that they might not see the
light of the gospel of the glory of Christ,
who is the image of God.*

Jesus said that the adoptive father of Adam's race was the devil.

*John 8:   44 "You are of your father the
devil, and you want to do the desires of
your father. He was a murderer from the
beginning, and does not stand in the
truth, because there is no truth in him.
Whenever he speaks a lie, he speaks from
his own nature; for he is a liar, and the
father of lies.*

We must understand that Satan's work is much more comprehensive than we have thought. You personally are talking to people every day who are highly influenced by demons, especially in certain segments of their life. These are demons who have taken advantage of the weakness of the sinful nature. These are demonic powers holding people in bondage.

- Ask God to expose and reveal the demons that have oppressed you.
- Jot these insights down.
- Rebuke and cast out the demon powers that have bound and opposed you.
- Ask God to show you demonic powers that oppress others around you.
- Through prophetic intercession command these spirits of torment and bondage to release people.

Don't give up after just one assault of rebuke. Don't be weary in the process of getting people free.

Remember Elijah commanded the Rain to come until it came.

Keep commanding bondage's to be broken until you see the evidence that it's happened.

#3. DISPLACING RULING DEMONS.

Strongs defines Rulers: 2888. kosmokrator, kos-mok-rat'-ore; from G2889 and G2902; a world-ruler, an epithet of Satan:--ruler.

- These are the demons who seek to promote the agenda of Satan in the earth. These we spiritual rulers are the demons in charge of the systems of the Kingdom of Darkness.

I would suggest that these demons preside over some of the following institutions. Presiding to influence or dominate.

- The Stock market
- The Drug cartel
- The Slave Trade
- The Mafia
- Gambling
- The Alcohol Industry
- Secular psychology, Psychiatry, Evolution theory, etc.
- The ACLU
- World Religions
- Certain dead Christian denominations
- Unions
- Education policy
- Banking, finance and commerce

These are the spirits who press the chosen agenda of the principalities into the mainstream of culture and society.

All these levels describe the forces of depravity.

Strong's defines "Wickedness in the heavenlies": 189. poneria, pon-ay-ree'-ah; from G4190; depravity, i.e. (spec.) malice; plur. (concr.) plots, sins:--iniquity, wickedness.

- Wicked plans and wicked influences that pervade the heavenlies adjacent to the earth realm. "Woe to the earth and it's inhabitants, for Satan has been cast down to the earth." (Revelation 12:12)

If you are walking in the light, keeping yourself in faith and confessing your sins, then you are "abiding in Him." You are seated "in Christ" at the right hand of the Father, in the heavenlies. In that case, all of these spirits are under your authority.

Remember you are a Deputy Sheriff under the authority of Sheriff Jesus. It's very important that you study the law book, the revised code of the Kingdom of Heaven...the Bible.

If you know the code book, you'll be able to stop the devil as he continually breaks the God's law of love and truth.

Jesus said, "All authority in heaven and in earth has been given to me". (Matthew 28:18) And then He said, "as the Father has sent me, so send I you." (John 20:21) So since you are in Him and commissioned by Him...what's under your authority?

What's in your specific jurisdiction or sphere of ministry calling?

Where is your ministry or influence needed?

How will you begin to use this truth with regard to government?

How has this book affected your prayer life and the way you'll use the Word of God?

#4. PLUNDERING SATAN'S HOUSE AND CALLING IN THE HARVEST.

Jeremiah 50: 2 "Declare and proclaim among the nations. Proclaim it and lift up a standard. Do not conceal it but say, 'Babylon has been captured, Bel has been put to shame, Marduk has been shattered; Her images have been put to shame, her idols have been shattered.'
Isaiah 43:5 "Do not fear, for I am with you; I will bring your offspring from the east, And gather you from the west. 6 "I will say to the north, 'Give them up!' And to the south, 'Do not hold them back.' Bring My sons from afar, And My daughters from the ends of the earth, 7 Everyone who is called by My name, And whom I have created for My glory, Whom I have formed, even whom I have made." 8 Bring out the people who are blind, even though they have eyes, And the deaf, even

though they have ears.

Psalm 149:5 Let the godly ones exult in glory; Let them sing for joy on their beds. 6 Let the high praises of God be in their mouth, And a two-edged sword in their hand,
7 To execute vengeance on the nations, And punishment on the peoples; 8 To bind their kings with chains, And their nobles with fetters of iron; 9 To execute on them the judgment written; This is an honor for all His godly ones. Praise the LORD!

John 4:35 "Do you not say, 'There are yet four months, and then comes the harvest'? Behold, I say to you, lift up your eyes, and look on the fields, that they are white for harvest.

Isaiah 62:6 On your walls, O Jerusalem, I have appointed watchmen; All day and all night they will never keep silent. You who remind the LORD, take no rest for yourselves; 7 And give Him no rest until He establishes And makes Jerusalem a praise in the earth.

Please write us or email us and give us some feedback to the good things that God does in your life as you implement these truths.

22489916R00132

Made in the USA
San Bernardino, CA
13 January 2019